A BOOK TO DIE FOR

A practical study guide on how our Bible came to us

WILLIAM J. McRAE

CLEMENTS PUBLISHING
Toronto

Published 2002 by Clements Publishing
6021 Yonge Street, Box 213
Toronto, Ontario M2M 3W2 Canada
www.clementspublishing.com

Scripture quotations are from the New American Standard Bible (NASB) unless
otherwise stated.

Cover image: "Impression of William Tyndale translating the Bible in prison,
1535" by Sabrina Low. Used by permission.
Cover design by Rob Clements

National Library of Canada Cataloguing in Publication Data

McRae, William J.
  A Book to Die For

  Rev. and expanded ed.
  First ed. published under title: The Birth of the Bible.
  Includes bibliographical references and index.

  ISBN 1-894667-13-1

  1. Bible—Inspiration. 2. Bible—Evidences, authority, etc. 3. Bible—Study and
teaching. I. McRae, William J. Birth of the Bible.
II. Title.

BS445.   M28 2002 220.1'3   C2002-900555-8

TABLE OF CONTENTS

ॐ

FOREWORD

꙳

William McRae plunges powerfully into the life of William Tyndale at the very point at which it is about to be extinguished, yet that death is about to bring Tyndale's life to its very fruition. Tyndale's poignant plea to his Lord to "open the King of England's eyes" is answered when, within two years, the English Bible, of which Tyndale has contributed seventy percent, is to be made available, indeed at the king's order, to all in each parish. The King of Kings has opened the eyes of the King of England!

Tyndale's strongest desire, even as a young man, was to bring the Word of God to every English man, woman and child in their own tongue in order that all may understand God's loving purposes for each. It is this pilgrimage that our author follows with faithfulness and care, but also with passion!

The story of Tyndale's life, short as it was, is told in sections, each focusing upon an important stage:

1. His education.
2. His attempt to receive ecclesiastical patronage, and therefore an opportunity to translate into the "vulgar tongue" while in his beloved country.
3. His disappointment and his consequent translation work in a number of European states, always harassed, once shipwrecked and driven hither and yon by the papal hounds.
4. His printings of the New Testament, the smuggling of these across the English Channel and the distribution of the Word, with its accompanying danger.
5. The cowardly betrayal of him, his following imprisonment and his ultimate trial and death.

The author continues by affirming William Tyndale's great God-given skill in languages and in translation, his brilliant theological knowledge and understanding, his lucid (and sometimes sharp) controversies with Sir Thomas More, and his effect upon the early English Reformers. This is the story of a remarkable but little-known man, master of seven languages and of matchless sensitivity in his translation from the original tongues of the Bible into the daily converse of the common man — a converse that is made use of even today. This hero is clearly admired and carefully described by the author in this brief prologue.

—Carrington (Tony) Tyndale
(A grateful descendant of William's brother,
Edward, through thirteen generations)

ACKNOWLEDGEMENTS

This volume represents a revision and expansion of an earlier book published under the title *The Birth of The Bible* in 1984. The occasion for this printing is the renaming of Ontario Bible College and Ontario Theological Seminary to Tyndale College & Seminary in May, 1998.

To commemorate this transition our President, Dr. Brian C. Stiller, has asked me to update my work on how our Bible came to us and to feature the contribution of William Tyndale. I am grateful for the encouragement and support of the Board of Governors and administration of the College and Seminary for this project.

The overview of the process of how our Bible came to us is adapted from a chart prepared by my good friend and seminary classmate, Pastor Michael Andrus of Manchester, Missouri. An expanded version is developed in his unpublished notes on "The Doctrine of Scripture."

I particularly appreciate two of my colleagues, Dr. Jim Beverley and Dr. John Vissers, who have read Chapter 4, "Inerrancy," and offered helpful suggestions on the current discussions on inerrancy.

Dr. Tony Tyndale, (now with the Lord), thirteenth-generation descendant of William Tyndale's brother, most graciously provided resource material on William Tyndale, reviewed the prologue, "William Tyndale: The Father of the English Bible," and wrote the foreword.

Several people have invested many hours in the preparation of this manuscript: my wife Marilyn and Mrs. Janice Ball, typing; Audrey Dorsch, editing; Helen Hofstetter and Ruth Whitt, administration and assistance. For the skills and management of each one I am most grateful. Rob Clements, of Clements Publishing, has been enormously helpful.

A special thanks to Brian Burnet, Louis Eizenga, John Harlton and Gordon Weber, close friends who have made possible the publishing of this book.

PROLOGUE

ಇ

WILLIAM TYNDALE:
THE FATHER OF THE ENGLISH BIBLE

"Lord, open the king of England's eyes."

Those were his last words. This was his last prayer.

The date is October 6, 1536. The location is the town of Vilvoorde, near Brussels in Belgium. The occasion is the execution of William Tyndale, age 42. One historian re-enacts the scene for us.

> The sun had barely risen above the horizon when he arrived at the open space, and looked out over the crowd of onlookers eagerly jostling for a good view. A circle of stakes enclosed the place of the execution, and in the center was a large pillar of wood in the form of a cross and as tall as a man.
>
> A strong chain hung from the top, and a noose of hemp was threaded through a hole in the upright. The attorney and the great doctors arrived first and seated themselves in state nearby. The prisoner was brought in and a final appeal was made that he should recant.
>
> Tyndale was immovable, his keen eyes gazing toward the common people. A silence fell over the crowd as they watched the prisoner's lean form and thin, tired face; his lips moved with a final impassioned prayer that echoed around the place of execution, "Lord, open the king of England's eyes."
>
> His feet were bound to the stake, the iron chain fastened around his neck, and the hemp noose was placed at his throat. Only the Anabaptists and lapsed heretics were burnt alive. Tyndale was spared that ordeal.
>
> Piles of brushwood and logs were heaped around him. The executioner came up behind the stake and with all his force snapped down upon the noose. Within seconds Tyndale was strangled.

The attorney stepped forward, placed a lighted torch to the tinder, and the great men and commoners sat back to watch the fire burn. Not until the charred form hung limply on the chain did an officer break out the staple of the chain with his halbert, allowing the body to fall into the glowing heat of the fire; more brushwood was piled on top and, while the commoners marveled "at the patient sufferance of Master Tyndale at the time of his execution," according to Foxe, the attorney and the doctors of Louvain moved off to begin their day's work, never imagining that within months at least part of the plea in Tyndale's dying prayer would be answered affirmatively.[1]

Who was this Tyndale and what had he done to warrant such violence?

He was faithful unto death. But why such injustice? What exactly was his crime? Was it worth it? What good did he really do? His life and times tell us the story.

TYNDALE'S LIFE AND TIMES

"If God spares my life, ere many years, I will cause a boy that driveth the plow shall know more of the Scriptures than thou dost."

Nothing more clearly defines the life and work of Tyndale than these words, spoken before he left England to undertake his life's work. Shocked by the ignorance of both the clergy and laity, he became convinced that only if the Scriptures were available to them in English would the people be established in the truth. The Bible of his day was in Latin, one thousand years old. Few understood it, read it or had access to it. The only English translation available was the hand-copied Wycliffe Bible that was secretly distributed by the Lollards, followers of the fourteenth-century John Wycliffe. But it had never been printed, and, having been translated only from the Latin Vulgate, it was inaccurate in many ways.

Herein lies Tyndale's greatest contribution. He profoundly influenced our history, becoming a major player in the great English Reformation. The English rapidly became a "people of the Book." That book was the Bible, translated, printed and distributed by Tyndale in the language of the people. We are enormously in his debt.

It is generally believed that it was about 1494 when William was born to a Tyndale family in Gloucestershire, near the Welsh border.

Our first hard facts locate him in Magdalen Hall, attached to Magdalen College of Oxford University, where he studied languages and theology, obtaining both his B.A. (1512) and M.A. (1515) before moving to Cambridge to continue his studies. It was here that his Protestant convictions were strengthened. He may well have participated in the lively discussions at The White Horse, the famous pub where Luther's theses of 1517 and subsequent articles were studied and debated. His name is associated here with Ridley,

Cranmer and Coverdale—all Cambridge men.

Dissatisfied with the teaching of theology at the universities, he left that world in 1521 and became a tutor in the household of Sir John Walsh at Little Sodbury Manor, near Bath. It was here that Tyndale was shocked by the biblical ignorance of the clergy. To one such cleric he declared, "If God spare my life, ere many years pass, I will cause a boy that driveth the plow shall know more of the Scriptures than thou dost."

Tyndale was beginning to clearly feel the call of God upon him to translate the Scriptures into English and distribute them to the common people.

This, however, was against the law. Because of the church's perceived threat from the Lollards, in 1408 the church banned the translation of the Bible into English.

It was a crime punishable by death. One day in 1519 the church authorities publicly burned a woman and six men for nothing more than teaching their children English versions of the Lord's Prayer, the Ten Commandments and the Apostle's Creed. In search of ecclesiastical approval, Tyndale obtained an interview with the bishop of London, Cuthbert Tunstall, but received no encouragement at all. Tyndale concluded, "[N]ot only was there no room in my lord of London's palace to translate the New Testament, but there was no place to do it in all of England."

Why such opposition? One historian writes:

> The church would never permit a complete printed New Testament in English from the Greek, because in that New Testament can be found neither the Seven Sacraments nor the doctrine of purgatory, two chief sources of the church's power.[2]

TYNDALE LEFT ENGLAND NEVER TO RETURN.

In April, 1524, Tyndale left England never to return. Supported by a group of wealthy London cloth merchants, he travelled to the Continent to engage in his work of translation.

Arriving in Hamburg, Germany, he worked on the New Testament, which was ready for printing the next year. The printing began in Cologne, only to be stopped by a police raid prompted by anti-reform church authorities. Fortunately Tyndale had been warned of the raid and fled just in time with the pages he had printed. A few fragments were left behind and confiscated. Only one copy of this incomplete edition has survived.

In 1526 Tyndale moved to Worms, a more secure and friendly city. Here the first complete New Testament in English was published. Of the 6,000 copies printed, only two have survived. One has been purchased by the British Library for one million pounds.

Getting the illegal New Testament into the hands of the English people was the next challenge. Fortunately there existed an established underground system for smuggling in censored books. They were shipped to England, hidden by dock workers in the cargo of English merchants who were sympathetic with the Reformation, then distributed in England by those merchants.

It is not surprising that so few copies survived. Church authorities did all they could to eradicate them. In 1526 the Bishop of London preached against the translation and had copies burned at St. Paul's Cathedral. In the following year the Bishop of London, encouraged by Augustine Packington, a friend of Tyndale's, bought copies of the New Testament and had them burned. Unknown to him, the substantial sums he paid provided Tyndale with funding to produce a better, more numerous second edition of his New Testament!

In 1530 Tyndale's translation of the Pentateuch was printed at Antwerp in Belgium, where he had settled, a centre like Cologne, which was a great port city with thriving trade lines to England. Here he continued his translation of the Old Testament and made several revisions of his New Testament. It also provided greater security for him . . . but only for a time.

TYNDALE'S ARREST AND TRIAL

> "Here thou hast (most dear reader) the new testament or covenant made with us of God in Christ's blood."
>
> Prologue
> Tyndale's Revised New Testament, 1534

For security reasons, in 1534 Tyndale moved into the home of Thomas Poyntz, a relative of Lady Walsh of Little Sodbury, an Englishman who kept a house of English merchants. Here Tyndale completed his most significant revision of the New Testament (1534). It is the New Testament as English readers and speakers have known it until the last few decades of the twentieth century.

While staying in Poyntz's home he befriended Henry Philips, an Oxford graduate who had fallen into extreme disgrace and poverty, then living in neighbouring Louvain. Louvain was a strong centre of Roman Catholicism and very antagonistic to the Reformation. Why did Philips now have sufficient money to enable him to live comfortably? Someone in London had paid him handsomely to carry out a secret operation of betrayal. He was to become like Judas, betraying his close friend.

En route to dinner together one day, Philips pointed with his finger over Tyndale's head, indicating to officers planted at the entrance to Poyntz's house whom they should arrest. Tyndale was imprisoned in the secure castle of Vilvoorde, six miles north of Brussels, eighteen miles from Antwerp, where he remained until his death.

In the following 450 days, evidence was gathered and charges were laid. For Tyndale those were long days of interrogation about his life, his beliefs and especially about his books and letters. Finally a formal accusation was prepared. Before seventeen commissioners Tyndale was charged with heresy, not agreeing with the Holy Roman Emperor.

In trapping Tyndale, his enemies had their biggest catch. He was a first class scholar, the prominent interpreter of Luther's ideas to the English and the major player in spreading the "heresy" of Lutheranism in London and across the entire country.

The decisive moment had come.

> The Biblical truths he had lived by for a dozen years of dangerous exile in poverty, which had driven his work of translating and writing with absolute dedication and total integrity . . . were not a matter of legal quibbles in an irregular court in a local spot in the Low Countries, but of Scripture itself, the Word of God *Himself.* [3] (emphasis added)

The issue at stake was a familiar one: salvation by faith alone, as Tyndale, Luther and the apostle Paul maintained, or salvation by works, as the Church of Rome insisted. Rather than acknowledge his "error," as he was expected to do, Tyndale dared to defend himself and was seen as unrepentant.

He was formally condemned as a heretic, degraded from the priesthood and handed over to the secular authorities for punishment—that is, burning at the stake. Each of these three phases were public events.

The condemnation for heresy included the public reading of the articles Tyndale had written declaring salvation by faith alone. In so doing, he demonstrated his disagreement with the Church of Rome.

The degradation of the priest followed a few days later:

> ... the prisoner was led on to a high platform, on which the bishops were prominent, in his priestly vestments. The anointing oil was symbolically scraped from his hands, the bread and wine of the Mass placed there and removed, and the vestments ceremonially stripped away.[4]

Two months later he was publicly executed, not by being burned alive, a terrible death often reserved for baser criminals, but by being strangled at the stake, after which his body was burned.

It is not without significance that the passion and purpose of his life was at the heart of his last spoken words before he was strangled: "Lord, open the king of England's eyes."

One year earlier, Miles Coverdale, Tyndale's friend, published the first ever complete printed edition of the Bible in English. For political reasons, Tyndale's name did not appear in it, though the translation was nearly seventy percent composed of Tyndale's work. God had already begun to answer Tyndale's last prayer.

Less than a year after Tyndale's martyrdom, King Henry VIII gave official approval of this Bible, and by 1539 every parish in England was required to make a copy of the English Bible available to all its people. Assured that the edition was free from heresies, Henry proclaimed, "Well, if there be no heresies in it, then let it be spread abroad among all the people!"

Tyndale had won![5]

TYNDALE'S LEGACY

> I beseeche you therefore brethren by the mercifulness of God, that ye make youre bodyes a quicke sacrifise, holy and acceptable unto God, which is youre resonable servynge off God. And fassion note youre selves lyke unto this worlde. But be ye chaunged [in youre shape] by the renuynge of youre wittes that ye may fele what thynge that good, that aceptable and perfaicte will of God is. (Rom. 12:1-2, 1526 edition)

THE TRANSLATOR

William Tyndale was many things, but first and foremost this man of God was a translator. This was his supreme gift. The consuming passion of his life was to provide a clear and accurate translation of the Scriptures in English for the common people to own and read. His greatest contribution then was his translation of Scripture for the first time, from the original Greek and Hebrew into English, and then printing it in pocket volumes for everyone to own.

His university education prepared him for this timely task. His skill in seven languages that he spoke like a native (Latin, Greek, Hebrew, Italian, Spanish, English and French) plus familiarity with German equipped him for his scholarly work. He had two working criteria: it had to be accurate and it had to make sense. In contrast to previous and subsequent versions, Tyndale is clear. He worked hard to speak the language of the people in a crisp, vivid, understandable style. "Fluent ease of expression in simple colloquial English are the conspicuous features of Tyndale's style."[6]

His New Testament translations include the Cologne Fragment (1525), The Worms New Testament (1526) and The Revised New Testament (1534). His Old Testament work resulted in three separate sections: The Pentateuch (1530), Jonah (1531) and selected passages from the Old Testament that were appointed to be read as epistles in the liturgy (1534), appended to his New Testament. There is tradition and evidence that he also translated Joshua to 2 Chronicles as found in Matthew's Bible of 1537.

The English Bible officially approved by Henry VIII within two years after Tyndale's death was nearly seventy percent composed of Tyndale's work. Ninety percent of his wording appeared in the King James Version published nearly 100 years later (1611). Seventy-five percent of his wording appeared in the Revised Standard Version of 1952.

C.H. Williams helps us understand the magnitude of Tyndale's influence when he writes,

> Tyndale's translations, together with the finest passages of his
> original writings, went into the making of modern English
> prose. Milton, Bunyan and a long list of later English writers
> were steeped in the language of the Authorized Version and in
> consequence, whether they knew it or not, they were debtors
> to the translator of the first New Testament. The ease with
> which the language of the Authorized Version became merged
> into the English heritage had paradoxical results. The sphere
> of Tyndale's influence was widened, but at the same time he
> was robbed of the recognition he deserved.... He found his
> surest triumph in the ascendancy of the 1611 text.[7]

The Reformer

Tyndale's influence as a translator was great but it was not immediate. His
Reformation writings, however, "were more immediately influential in mar-
shalling Protestant opinion in England."[8]

His influence came from both his own personal writings and his interpretation of Luther's ideas to English readers. The authorities recognized the
threat of these materials immediately and banned them in England by royal
proclamation.

Tyndale's first such work was the *Prologue to the Epistle to the Romans*,
probably printed in Worms (1525). One quarter is Tyndale's; the remainder is
Luther's. As expected, the subject is an exposition of justification by faith. It
found a ready sale in England but was loudly denounced by Sir Thomas More
and the authorities.

The Parable of the Wicked Mammon was his next venture (1528). The
theme is an exposition of the parable of the unjust steward (Luke 16). His
deeper interest in this exposition is once again the doctrine of justification by
faith alone.

In 1528 *The Obedience of the Christian Man* was published, the largest
and most important of his writings. It is a defence of the need to study the
Bible—all hope for the reformation of the church depends upon an awareness
of the errors in Roman theology and practice. "In his insistence on the lay-
man's right to read and interpret the Scriptures for himself, Tyndale was putting before his English readers the most radical challenge made in
Reformation thought."[9]

Here Tyndale argues that Christians have the duty of obedience to cruel
authorities, except where loyalty to God is concerned.

Despite it being illegal to possess a copy of this book, Lady Ann Boleyn
possessed a copy and passed it on to King Henry VIII, who loved it and said,
"This book is for me and all kings to read."

The Practice of the Prelates was the last of these writings (1530). "It is the most remarkable, and easily the most bitter of his polemical writings."[10] Tyndale's persecution has had its effect. His frustration is evident. It must be read against the dark background of the events in England during those years—Henry VIII's determination to force a papal decision on the legality of his first marriage. The writing contains "the first outpouring of Tyndale's pent-up thoughts about the Church of Rome, its claims to privilege, its teachings and the actions of its ministers."[11]

THE CONTROVERSIALIST

Tyndale's tumultuous life was punctuated by violent literary clashes with Sir Thomas More, the lord chancellor, commissioned by the king and the church to refute William Tyndale's arguments and to discredit his character.

Tyndale attacked the institutions of the Church of Rome, concentrating his attention on the errors and shortcomings of the clergy. Sir Thomas More responded with a personal attack on Tyndale's character. The battle intensified and deteriorated over the years (1529-1533) and yielded such writings as More's "Dialogue Concerning Heresies" (1529), Tyndale's "Answer To More" (1531), "More's Confutation" (1532-1533) and his "Apology" (1533).

For Sir Thomas More, the Roman Catholic Church was the true, infallible church. A heretic was anyone who opposed the church, its representatives and its teachings. Any such heretics he had burned at the stake. For Tyndale, the true and final authority was Scripture, and any person or group denying this was in league with Antichrist. It was this conviction that brought him to his violent death, but drove the movement we know as the Great English Reformation.

THE THEOLOGIAN

The starting point of Tyndale's religious thinking was his convictions that the Scriptures were both authoritative and adequate. Though to many evangelicals today these seem so elementary, in his day it was simply radical, opposing the humanism of Erasmus and the traditionalism of the church.

> He attacked the long established Roman method of Bible exegesis. It was based on the assumption that most sentences in the Bible could be interpreted in four senses. These were the literal sense, which explains the historical content of the text; the tropological sense, which teaches what we ought to do; the allegorical sense, which reveals the metaphorical implications of the text in order to explain matters of faith; and lastly there was the anagogical sense which dealt with the spiritual or mystical interpretation of the text. Tyndale accepted the literal sense of Scripture.[12]

This was absolutely decisive in determining the course of his life. Once he had made this decision about the authority and interpretation of the Bible, the die was cast. There could be no compromise. His break with Rome was inevitable. His death was certain.

Luther's influence on Tyndale's theology was significant indeed. Perhaps at Cambridge he had received his first exposure to Lutheranism. Certainly his stay in Wittenberg would have provided him many opportunities for direct contact with Luther and his doctrine. Luther's influence is evident in Tyndale's teaching of justification by faith alone and of the eucharist as a memorial—not a sacrifice. His *Brief Declaration* (1533) clearly presents his position.

More recent research, seeking to trace the origins of Puritan thought and theory, has led some scholars back to William Tyndale "in whose writings they found the germ of ideas which would later form the basis of Puritan theology."[13]

While opinions vary on the quality of Tyndale's theology, he was an important leader among those who shaped the thinking of the English Reformation.

THE POLITICAL AND SOCIAL CONSCIENCE

Though Tyndale's primary interests were in the realm of Bible translation and church reformation, by the nature of his times he was compelled to express his position on the great political and social issues of his day.

Were the reformers actually responsible for the unrest that was undermining the secular authorities in Europe, as was charged by church leaders? Tyndale answered this accusation in 1528 in *The Obedience of a Christian Man*. Here he argued that the doctrine of the reformers did not condone political unrest, but rather called for obedience to civil authorities, except where obedience to God is concerned. He maintained that the unrest and evils could actually be traced to the Roman church.

Two years later, in *The Practice of Prelates*, he explored in depth the relation of the church and state, an issue created by Henry VIII's determination to pursue the annulment of his marriage to Catherine. Here he also addressed various social issues, each from a strong biblical perspective such as the importance of vocation, the relationship between servant and master, the role of landlords and the problem of riches.

Through his writings Tyndale engaged his culture and addressed the pressing evils from a Christian perspective.

A MAN FOR OUR TIMES

Like Abel of old, through Tyndale's obedience, scholarship, character and sacrifice, "though he is dead, he still speaks" (Heb. 11:4).

Tyndale was a biblicist. In matters of faith and practice the Scriptures were his first and final authority. His personal faith rested entirely upon the Word of God. It was his faith in the power of the teachings of the Bible to regenerate sinners, reform the church and transform society that nurtured his passion and motivated his life. Today, when philosophy, psychology and sociology seem to dominate, we need to catch again his heartbeat and settled conviction for the trustworthiness, authority and sufficiency of Scripture.

He was also a student and scholar. God used his years of diligent study, careful research, insightful reflection, critical and constructive writing to further the work of God's kingdom. Today Tyndale stands as a model for Christians, young and old, of discipline, excellence, integrity and courage, when mediocrity is too often the standard.

He was a man of virtuous character. The case can be made that the closer his opponents came to know him, the deeper their respect grew for his character. Even the procurator-general spoke of him as "learned, godly and good." At a time when *education* and *giftedness* get top grades, we need once again to restore *character*, as seen in Tyndale, to its priority.

He was persecuted and martyred. He started well, he ran well and he finished well. He was faithful unto death. What he stood for incited fierce opposition and intense resistance, but he stood! Today we seem to have enshrined, as our fourth inalienable right, the right to be free from suffering, conflict, opposition and pain. Tyndale's life declares again that such circumstances are not only part of our calling, but often the crucible that serves to refine and release our distinctive gifts.

And finally, Tyndale's story also reminds us that Christians who set no limits on their dedication can have massive, positive influence on the powerful forces in control of societies. This is seen in the fact that Tyndale, who was once seen as the public's enemy, is today heralded as one of its greatest benefactors, and that the Bible in English is a recognized bestseller every year.[14]

And yet the Tyndale tale is not an isolated story. He was one of a mighty army of spiritual giants who participated in the remarkable drama of how we got our Bible. His is only one frame, especially enlarged in this prologue to commemorate the name change of Ontario Bible College and Ontario Theological Seminary to Tyndale College & Seminary, and to introduce him to a generation that needs to meet him and know him. May his life leave its mark on each of our students, staff and faculty. May we leave his mark on our generation.

The chapters that follow are devoted to the larger picture, stage by stage, of how we got this wonderful treasure we call *the Bible*.

END NOTES

[1] Brian Edwards, "Tyndale's Betrayal and Death," *Church History*, Volume VI, No.4, Issue 16, p.15.

[2] David Daniell, *William Tyndale, A Biography* (Yale University Press, New Haven & London, 1994), p.100.

[3] *Ibid.*, p.376.

[4] *Ibid.*, p.374.

[5] In this summary of Tyndale's life and times, arrest and trial, I am indebted to Tony Lane, professor of Bible at London Bible College, London, England, in "A Man For All People: Introducing William Tyndale," *Church History*, Volume VI, No.4, Issue 16, pp.6-9, and Brian Edwards, minister in Surrey, England, in "Tyndale's Betrayal and Death," *Church History*, Volume VI, No. 4, Issue 16, pp.12-15.

[6] C.H. Williams, *William Tyndale* (London: Thomas Nelson & Sons Ltd., 1969), p.80.

[7] *Ibid.*, pp.81,82.

[8] *Ibid.*, p.84.

[9] *Ibid.*, p.92.

[10] *Ibid.*, p.93.

[11] *Ibid.*, p.94.

[12] *Ibid.*, p.127.

[13] *Ibid.*, p.130.

[14] A.K. Curtis, "From The Publisher," *Church History*, Volume VI, No.4, Issue 16, p.2.

BIBLIOGRAPHY

Curtis, A.K. "William Tyndale." *Christian History*, Vol. VI, No.4, Issue 16, pp.2-35.

Daniell, David. *William Tyndale, A Biography*. New Haven and London: Yale University Press, 1994.

Douglas, J.D. (ed.). *The New International Dictionary of the Christian Church*. Grand Rapids, MI: Zondervan Publishing House, 1974.

Galli, Mark (ed.). "How We Got Our Bible." *Christian History*, Vol. XIII, No.3, Issue 43, pp.2-41.

Tenney, Merrill C. *The Zondervan Pictorial Encyclopedia of the Bible*. 5 Vols. Grand Rapids, MI: Zondervan Publishing House, 1975.

Williams, C.H. *William Tyndale*. London: Thomas Nelson and Sons, Ltd., 1969.

INTRODUCTION

ॐ

A curious Hindu lady, sitting with us in the living room of a mutual friend, asked, "Isn't the Bible just one among many sacred books in the world today?" After a home Bible study class, a deeply concerned Dallas executive asked, "Why do you believe the Bible?" A rather skeptical young woman at The University of Texas in Austin challenged me during an evening rap session with the question, "How do you know the Bible is really true?" These are questions that cannot be avoided. They deserve honest answers. But what are the answers?

It must be acknowledged, of course, that each of the eleven living world religions has a definite set of documents that is regarded as conveying unique divine truth needed for man's salvation. The Qur'an of the Muslims and the Vedas of the Hindus both have a theory of verbal inspiration and literal infallibility. The sacred book of each of these religions claims to be pre-eminent. Shintoism's Ko-ji-ki says, "There is none among the writings in the world so noble and so important as this classic."

For a moment this seems to settle the point. The Bible is simply one among many sacred books. Yet that is not so. It stands apart from every other book. It is unique and its uniqueness lies in four areas.

It is unique in its moral and ethical standards. The morality and ethics of the Bible are far superior to those of any other sacred book. The "god" of the Qur'an is a "god who deceives people." Their "heaven" is a place of sensual living: eating, drinking and maidens. Why is this significant? Such concepts reflect the base nature of humanity and human instincts. On the other hand, only too well we know that the holiness, justice and love of the God of the Bible, as well as the total absence of the sensual in God's heaven, reflect concepts that are very foreign to our nature.

Add to this the uniqueness of the message of salvation the Bible proclaims to mankind. A Hindu may choose to pursue one of three ways of works to obtain salvation. A Buddhist is a lamp unto oneself and seeks for salvation through works. A Muslim must obey the "Five Pillars" of Islam to reach Paradise. And so it is with the religions of the world. The salvation of every individual rests either partially or totally with that person. Salvation is a process dependent upon the works of the individual. Not so in the Bible. Salvation is an act of God apart from our own works. Humans are totally lost, incapable of doing anything toward our salvation. We are entirely shut up to the grace of God. Unparalleled in all religious literature are these majestic words:

> For by grace are ye saved through faith: and that not of yourselves, it is the gift of God: Not of works, lest any man should boast. (Eph. 2:8,9)

But we have only begun. For many people the most persuasive fact pointing to the uniqueness of the Bible is that the Bible alone places upon itself a test. According to Deuteronomy 18:20-22, that test is the accurate fulfillment of prophecy:

> But the prophet who shall speak a word presumptuously in My name which I have not commanded him to speak, or which he shall speak in the name of other gods, that prophet shall die.

> And you may say in your heart, "How shall we know the word which the Lord has not spoken?"

> When a prophet speaks in the name of the Lord, if that thing does not come about or come true, that is the thing which the Lord has not spoken. The prophet has spoken it presumptuously; you shall not be afraid of him.

It is in fulfillment of a prophetic utterance that the truthfulness of the prophet is affirmed.

Philip Mauro observed the significance of this test a number of years ago when, in the introduction to John Urquhart's *The Wonders of Prophecy,* he said:

> Let it be remembered that one of the most striking characteristics of the Bible, distinguishing it radically from all other books either ancient or modern, is that it contains in every part, from the third chapter of Genesis to the last of Revelation, predictions in plain language of events that were to take place in the history of mankind on earth.

> Let it be remembered too, that the prophecies of the Bible are not confined to small, local affairs, but have for their subjects the most important countries of the world, the most famous nations and empires, the greatest cities.

> Had history falsified those prophecies, or any of them, the enemies of the Bible would have put the facts in evidence. Stupendous efforts have been made to prove error in statements of the Bible, whether in regard to facts of nature or facts of history. But here is a field—prophecy—which is both long and wide, and abounds in statements on many subjects.

A field in which, if the statements had been those of men,
would contain as many errors as predictions; and yet the
enemies of the Bible do not attempt to impeach it for false
prophecies.*

Have you ever heard the veracity of the Bible challenged on the grounds
of false prophecy? Yet that is the test the Bible places upon itself. No other
sacred book dares to subject itself to such a potentially dangerous test.

But to leave the question at this point is to offer an incomplete answer.

The distinctiveness of the Bible rests not only upon its moral and ethical
standards, its message of salvation, its test of fulfilled prophecy, but also on the
nature and extent of its claim for itself.

It claims to be a direct revelation from God! True, other books claim verbal inspiration, infallibility and divine authority. But no other book makes the
kind of claim the Bible makes for itself. Its claim is not based upon a single
proof text, nor upon a creedal statement of a church council. It permeates
every page of Scripture. No other book has that kind of evidence to support
its claim. In the pages that follow, witnesses will be called from six major areas
to support its claim.

Among the sacred books of the world, the Bible stands absolutely unique.

A defence of the uniqueness of the Bible, however, only proves that the
Bible is unique. It proves nothing more. To answer the challenges raised
against its claim for itself and our claims for it, more information, much more
information, is needed. It is to meet this need that this book is offered both to
the Christian and non-Christian world.

It is my personal conviction that nothing will prepare a person more for
the defence of the Bible than a clear understanding of the historical process
whereby the Bible came to us. Hopefully, the pages that follow will equip each
of us to be more effective defenders of our faith.

---

* John Urquhart, *The Wonders of Prophecy* (Harrisburg, PA: Christian Publications, Inc., 1925), viii, ix.

AN OVERVIEW OF THE PROCESS
&
HOW WE GOT OUR BIBLE

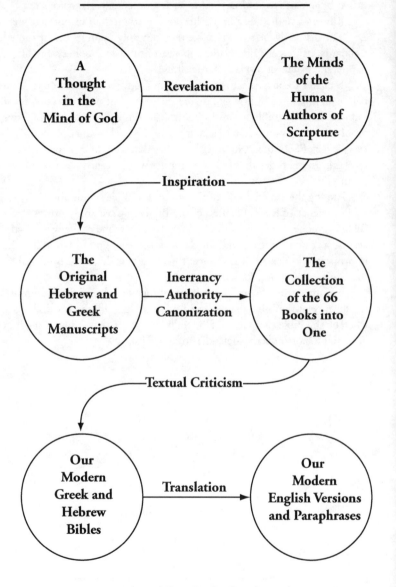

Adapted from Michael Andrus

Part I

ॐ

REVELATION

CHAPTER ONE

THE CHALLENGE

Preparing the Way

Can you answer these questions? Try them.

1. What is the meaning of the words "reveal" and "revelation" as they are used in our Bible?

2. Man is entirely dependent upon revelation from God for his knowledge in at least four major areas. What are they?

3. What is the distinction between general and special revelation?

4. General revelation comes to all men via three channels. Can you name them and support each one with Scripture?

5. Where and when only is special revelation found?

Now for some answers!

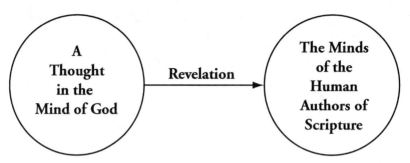

One of the most exciting ministries God has ever entrusted to me was the privilege of teaching a Bible class for the members of the Dallas Cowboys football team. For two years we met each Wednesday night in the home of one of the players. What the class lacked in numbers, it more than made up in interest and controversy. Every class was an adventure. Week after week I faced men who seemed half my age but twice my size. Among them were some of the finest men I have ever met. They were men who struggled not only with fame and fortune, but also with the same deep personal problems that plague you and me. Some of the most stimulating hours of my entire life were spent in their company.

We began the class with an eight-week series entitled, *God's Plan for The Ages*. I shall never forget the first night as long as I live. My wife and I arrived early, slightly nervous but very excited. We prayed together with the player and his wife who had opened their home for the class. We were trusting God to bring just the right men and their wives to the class and to have the right message for each of them. After a few uneasy moments, the first couple arrived. I stood before one of the finest ball players in the NFL. When he asked what we were actually going to be doing I explained that we would simply be studying what the Bible says about God's plan for the ages. He confessed he had never before studied the Bible.

After that first class, one of the players lingered into the early hours of the morning, asking question after question that probed the deepest issues of life and drove us over and over again into the Scriptures.

If that first night is the most memorable, a very close second came just a few weeks later. That night an all-star lineman came to the class for the first time. After the study he took me back to square one and challenged the Bible.

Being an intellectual type, he had just read *The Chariot of the Gods*. He was impressed with the possibilities presented in the book. In his opinion it offered an explanation of our origins that had solid scientific support. Surrounded by his teammates, equipped with a sharp mind and armed with an arsenal of arguments, he stated his challenge succinctly, "How do you know the Bible is true?"

Here is a challenge that sooner or later will face every Christian who dares to live in the arena of real life. It is a challenge that cannot be ignored. It demands an honest reply. Do you have one?

To answer the questions we must understand, first of all, the historical process of how our Bible came to us. The initial step in this process is the revelation of truth, which God gave to man. It is revelation that bridges the gap between a thought in the mind of God and the minds of human authors of Scripture.

It is this step, this bridge — revelation — that is to be mastered in our first two chapters.

I. The Term

Revelation is simply the work of God communicating to men truth that was previously unknown and unknowable through any other means (Eph. 3:5,6; Gal. 1:12; 1 Pet. 1:12).

II. Our Fourfold Need for Revelation

A few years ago a professor in the medical school of a large Canadian university startled his class with this statement, "It is impossible for a human to know what God is really like." He was expressing the frustration of a finite man trying to comprehend an infinite God. Of course it is impossible if we are going from the creature to the Creator.

But reverse the process for a moment. Go from God to man and it is no longer impossible. For our knowledge of God we are entirely dependent upon the self-revelation of God. We can know nothing of God apart from what He uncovers of Himself to us.

The famed reformed theologian L. Berkhof establishes a crucial distinction at this point. Referring to a contemporary he notes,

> Kuyper calls attention to the fact that theology as the knowledge of God differs in an important point from all other knowledge. In the study of all other sciences man places himself above the object of his investigation and actively elicits from it his knowledge by whatever method may seem most appropriate, but in theology he does not stand above but rather under the object of his knowledge. In other words, men can know God only insofar as the latter actually makes Himself known.[1]

Just as no one really knows you except your own personal spirit, so no one knows God except the Spirit of God. He it is who knows Him thoroughly, and He it is who reveals Him to us (1 Cor. 2:10,11). Without that revelation it is indeed impossible for a person to know what God is really like. Our first need for revelation is for knowledge of God. But that is not all.

The Apollo flights are now history. One of the announced objectives of their exploration was to search the moon for answers to the origins of humanity and the universe. The long search for our origins has been an expensive and exhausting enterprise. The product has only borne out what a noted British scientist, Lord Kelvin, said a number of years ago, "There is nothing in science that reaches the origin of anything at all."

Once again we are shut up to revelation. Theories come and hypotheses go but the question of origins remains unanswered by philosophy and science. Sir William Dawson, Canadian geologist, summed it all up when he said, "I know nothing about the origin of man except what I am told in the Scriptures that God created him. I do not know anything more than that and I do not know anybody who does." In our search for our own origins lies our second need for revelation.

But come from the distant past to the clamouring present for our third need. What is our responsibility to God today? Surely we will agree that we have some responsibility to Him. If there is a God, and if we are the creatures of God, then it follows that we are responsible to Him. What is that responsibility?

How futile and arrogant it is for humans to attempt to devise ethical codes or religious systems and impose them upon ourselves. It is as ridiculous as an employee determining one's responsibility to an employer, an individual citizen assessing one's own obligation to the state or a student deciding one's responsibility to the professors (which in some cases is no longer ridiculous). As the responsibility of the employee, citizen and student is determined by the one to whom the person is responsible, so our responsibility to God is determined by Him alone.

But how is it known? Only by revelation. God Himself must make it known to us. The syllabus of a course, the student handbook for dormitory residents, the orientations at college are all designed to inform the students of their responsibilities. The administration has a moral obligation to tell the students such things if they are to be held responsible for them. Almighty God has a similar moral obligation to disclose to us the nature of our responsibility to Him. Once again we become very conscious of our tremendous need of divine revelation.

This is just as true of a fourth sphere. There never has been a time when there has been more interest in the future than today. Twelve million copies of *The Late Great Planet Earth* were printed in its first eleven years. Millions of Americans read their horoscopes, thousands consult mediums and dabble in the occult, all in an attempt to probe the future. There is something about our age that makes us ask as never before, Where are we going?

Since the eighteenth-century enlightenment, many attempts have been made to find some goal in the historical process. After reviewing the philosophies of history formulated by Kant, Hegel, Marx, Spengler and Toynbee, Dr. John W. Montgomery concludes,

> No man, from the secular, humanistic viewpoint, can answer
> the question "Where is history going?" All of us, to use Jack

Kerouac's phrase, are "on the road" and our historical search-lights are incapable of illuminating all of the path we have traversed. They continually meet a wall of fog ahead of us.[2]

The only meaningful and conclusive answer to the question of ultimate values and eternal destinies must come from One who is above and outside the historical process. For knowledge of the future, our fourth need, we are shut up to divine revelation.

Do we need it? Without it we can know nothing of God. Without it our origins are buried in the murky waters of the past. Without it we flounder with no idea of our responsibility to our God. Without it history has no goal and life has no purpose.

The very central contention of Christianity is that God graciously and satisfactorily met every one of these needs through revelation. This revelation has come in a variety of forms.

III. Two Major Classifications

By a careful consideration of the subject matter revealed and the manner of revelation, it is possible to speak of revelation in terms of two major classifications: general and special.

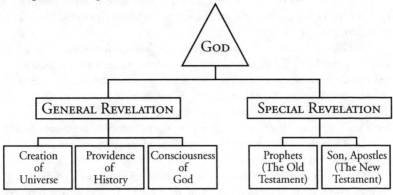

A. General Revelation

This is the divine testimony to the existence and character of God given to all people by means of creation, providence and conscience. It is discerned by human reason. It was designed to lead people, as they were created, to an enjoyment of the knowledge of God.

1. CREATION

The heavens are telling of the glory of God; And their expanse is declaring the work of His hands. Day to day pours forth speech, And night to night reveals knowledge. (Ps. 19:1,2)

> Because that which is known about God is evident within
> them, for God made it evident to them. For since the cre-
> ation of the world His invisible attributes, His eternal power
> and divine nature, have been clearly seen, being understood
> through what has been made, so that they are without excuse.
> (Rom. 1:19,20)

The creation of God testifies to the existence of God and His character. The greatness of creation reveals His eternal power. The orderliness of creation reveals His divine nature.

2. PROVIDENCE

> And yet He did not leave Himself without witness, in that He
> did good and gave you rains from heaven and fruitful seasons
> satisfying your hearts with food and gladness. (Acts 14:17)

The rains are providential acts of God, revealing His goodness to all peo-
ple. Without them there would be no crops, no harvests and no food. By the way, this is why a Christian gives thanks to God for his food.

3. CONSCIOUSNESS OF GOD

> Then God said, "Let Us make man in Our image, according
> to Our likeness, and let them rule over the fish of the sea and
> over the birds of the sky and over the cattle and over all the
> earth, and over every creeping thing that creeps on the
> earth." (Gen. 1:26)

One aspect of being in the image of God is the human consciousness of God. Marred as the image was by the fall of man in the Garden of Eden, something of it is still retained in fallen humanity (1 Cor. 11:7; James 3:9). Historically there has been a consciousness of a Supreme Being in all people, among all tribes and peoples, which has been expressed in some form of religious life.

The courageous story of Helen Keller has thrilled the hearts of thousands. Although Keller was born deaf, a very patient teacher taught her to talk. After some time the teacher thought she should be taught about God, so invited Philip Brooks to come and teach her. As far as the teacher knew, this was the first time Keller had heard about God. Upon hearing, Keller said she always knew there was a God, but didn't know His name. There is this consciousness of God in every person.

Several years ago our six-year old daughter confounded her father by ask-
ing if God had a birthday party. When I said, "I seriously doubt it," she replied, "If He does, I sure hope He invites me sometime. I'd really like to know what He looks like!"

In general revelation we have quite a portrait of God. But it is only a partial picture!

B. Special Revelation

This is the divine testimony to God's plan of salvation given to sinners —
through the prophets of God and through the Son of God.

This is embodied in the Scriptures and is comprehended by faith alone.

> Many other signs therefore Jesus also performed in the pres-
> ence of the disciples, which are not written in this book; but
> these have been written that you may believe that Jesus is the
> Christ, the Son of God; and that believing you may have life
> in His name. (John 20:30,31)

There are two distinct phases in the special revelation given to us by God
in the Scriptures. The Old Testament is preparatory and anticipatory, with a
focus on the nation of Israel and the Abrahamic and Mosaic covenants. The
New Testament records the fulfillment of God's plan of redemption and the
consummation of the ages. Its focus is on the church and the new covenant.

> God, after He spoke long ago to the fathers in the prophets
> in many portions and in many ways, in these last days has
> spoken to us in His Son. . . . (Heb. 1:1-2a)

Special revelation radiates the righteousness, grace and love of God. This
not only completes the picture, but sharpens the focus on general revelation.
This was observed by John Calvin, who said, "In the Bible we have the Divine
spectacles which bring the truths of natural theology into focus." Pascal noted
the remarkable relationship between general and special revelation when he
said, "Just as all things speak of God to those who know Him and unveil Him
to those who love Him, even so they hide Him from those who neither seek
Him nor know Him."

Mark this well: General revelation is never sufficient to save a man.
Salvation is only through a personal faith in Jesus Christ who has died as our
substitute, bearing our sin in His own body on the cross. In His death He
bore the punishment for our sin and fully satisfied the righteous demands of
God for the payment of sin. Because sin has been judged and punished in
Jesus Christ, God is righteously able to forgive all who receive Christ as their
personal Saviour. There is no salvation apart from trusting in Him. This is
known only by special revelation.

> I am the way, the truth, and the life; no one comes to the
> Father, but through Me. (John 14:6)

> There is salvation in no one else; for there is no other name
> under heaven that has been given among men, by which we
> must be saved. (Acts 4:12)

Although general revelation is not sufficient to save, it is sufficient to condemn. Because of it, " . . . they are without excuse" (Rom. 1:20). To reject God's revelation of Himself in creation, providence and conscience is to bring condemnation.

The contrasts between the two major classifications of revelation can be simply charted.

General	Special
1. Testimony to the existence and character of God.	1. Testimony to the plan of salvation.
2. Testimony to all people.	2. Testimony to sinners.
3. Discovered by human reason.	3. Discerned by faith.
4. Designed to lead us to enjoy God.	4. Designed to lead us to salvation.
5. This revelation condemns.	5. This revelation saves.

It is special revelation that will occupy our attention in this book — the revelation through the prophets and the Son, which is contained in the Word of God.

This is why men and women down through the centuries have read it, studied it, loved it, preached it, lived by it and died for it. The Bible is the Word of God.

But is it really? That is the challenge before us. With this background we are now prepared to respond. Before we answer the challenge however, it will be well to pause and review.

Review

This chapter began with five questions. Turn back to "Preparing the Way" at the beginning of this chapter and go over the questions once more. Be sure you are able to answer each one correctly. An understanding of these concepts is basic to answering the challenge.

FOR FURTHER STUDY

"Although general revelation is not sufficient to save, it is sufficient to condemn!"

Relate this statement to the question of those who have never heard of Jesus Christ. How does God deal with men and women who are without special revelation?

END NOTES

[1] L. Berkhof, *Systematic Theology* (Grand Rapids, MI; Wm. B. Eerdmans Publishing Company, 1908), p.34.

[2] John Montgomery, "The Current Muddle Over History," *HIS*, April, 1971, p.29.

BIBLIOGRAPHY

Dewitt, David A. *Answering the Tough Ones*. Chicago, IL: Moody Press, 1980, p.135.

Henry, Carl F. H. (ed.). *Revelation and the Bible*. Grand Rapids, MI: Baker Book House, 1958, p.413.

Pinnock, Clark. *Biblical Revelation*. Chicago, IL: Moody Press, 1971, p.256.

CHAPTER TWO

૭ૢ

ANSWERING THE CHALLENGE

Preparing the Way

1. In what three ways does the Bible claim to be a direct revelation from God?

2. In what sense can we say all the Bible is a revelation of God, even parts recorded by eyewitnesses?

3. What evidence is there that Genesis 1-11 is historically accurate and reliable, and not mythological?

4. Any book, of course, can claim to be a revelation of God. What evidence is there to support this claim of the Bible?

5. Explain: The Bible is not the kind of book men would write if they could; nor is it the kind of book men could write if they would.

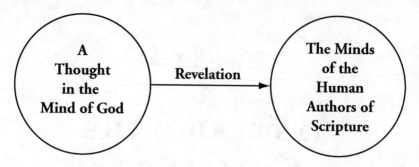

How do you know the Bible is true? How do *you* know the Bible is true? How do you know the *Bible* is true? How do you know the Bible is *true*? Regardless of where the emphasis falls, the question is a challenge. The small huddle of football players and wives who attended that Bible class in Dallas waited for an answer.

I simply said, "I know the Bible is true because it is a revelation from God."

But this is hardly sufficient. How can we demonstrate that it is, indeed, a revelation from God?

The Bible: A Divine Revelation

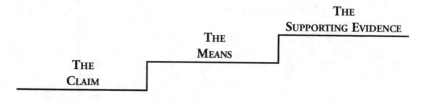

I. The Claim

One of the surest things to be said about the Bible is that it claims to be a divine revelation. This is expressed in at least three ways.

A. By Its Direct Statements

More than 3,800 times the claim that the Bible is a revelation of God occurs in phrases with the ring of a "thus saith the Lord."

The first such statement occurs in Genesis 15:1, "After these things the word of the Lord came to Abram in a vision, saying, . . ." In 1 Kings 17:14, Elijah the prophet says, "For thus says the lord God of Israel, . . ." David declares in Psalm 103:7, "He made known His ways to Moses, His acts to the sons of Israel." Many other verses speak to this point. "God, after He spoke long ago to the fathers in the prophets in many portions and in many ways, in these last days has spoken to us in His Son, whom He appointed heir of all things, through whom also He made the world" (Heb. 1:1,2). "For this we say to you by the word of the Lord, . . ." (1 Thess. 4:15). "For I received from the Lord that which I also delivered to you, that the Lord Jesus in the night in which He was betrayed took bread . . ." (1 Cor. 11:23). "As He spoke by the mouth of His holy prophets from of old . . ." (Luke 1:70). "And Moses wrote down all the words of the lord. Then he arose early in the morning, and built an altar at the foot of the mountain with twelve pillars for the twelve tribes of Israel" (Ex. 24:4). "Thus says the lord the God of Israel, 'Write all the words which I have spoken to you in a book'" (Jer. 30:2). "Then the lord stretched out His hand and touched my mouth, and the lord said to me, 'Behold, I have put My words in your mouth'" (Jer. 1:9). "Which things we also speak, not in words taught by human wisdom, but in those taught by the Spirit, combining spiritual thoughts with spiritual words" (1 Cor. 2:13).

It is not the dogma of a denomination or the claim of the creed. It is not an isolated text or a veiled illusion. The entire Bible is permeated with direct statements that it is a divine revelation.

B. By Attributing the Words of Men to God

Frequently the Scriptures actually attribute to God words that men have previously spoken. This is a much more subtle claim to revelation but it cannot be avoided. From many possible examples consider the one in Hebrews 1:7: "And of the angels He says, 'Who makes His angels winds, And His ministers a flame of fire.'"

Here the author of the epistle to the Hebrews quotes from Psalm 104:4, obviously written originally by the psalmist. But wait a moment. Our text reads, "And of the angels *He says* ..." (emphasis added). The antecedent of this pronoun is God, as is clear from the preceding six verses. Here is no small claim! The writer attributes to God the words of the psalmist. This illustration could be multiplied by the dozens from the pages of Scripture.

C. By Our Lord's Attitude toward the Old Testament

Surely one of the Bible's most forceful claims to divine revelation is our Lord's attitude toward the Scriptures. If He is to be believed, His attitude must be respected.

He authenticates the Old Testament Scriptures by His word.

> Do not think that I came to abolish the Law or the Prophets; I did not come to abolish, but to fulfill.
>
> For truly I say to you, until heaven and earth pass away, not the smallest letter or stroke shall pass away from the Law, until all is accomplished. (Matt. 5:17,18)

He authenticates it, further, by His life. In approaching the cross, He said, "The Son of Man is to go, just as it is written of Him ..." (Matt. 26:24). Here is a clear confession of His recognition of the Old Testament as divine revelation.

Reflecting upon His crucifixion, He said:

> These are My words which I spoke to you while I was still with you, that all things which are written about Me in the Law of Moses and the Prophets and the Psalms must be fulfilled.

> Then He opened their minds to understand the Scriptures, and He said to them, "Thus it is written, that the Christ should suffer and rise again from the dead the third day; ..." (Luke 24:44-46)

What remarkable words! Here is His stamp of certification upon the Scriptures of the Old Testament. He acknowledges that they were a divine revelation not only in His teaching, but also in His living. He ordered the details of His life according to the Scriptures.

In one form or another the claim appears on virtually every page of Scripture. It is impossible to escape the fact that the Bible claims to be a revelation of God. This was the point I made with my challenger. I believe the Bible to be true because it claims to be a revelation from God.

To assert that, in its entirety, the Bible is a revelation from God is to arouse the critics with their guns loaded. In unison the skeptics of the Scriptures scream out against the early chapters of Genesis. Here are events that, if true, could only be known by revelation. But today the historicity of those chapters is jettisoned in favour of a mythological interpretation. Yet the evidence from the Bible is that these chapters are historical and the contents were known by revelation.

John Gerstner has marshalled a convincing list of evidences:

> First, on the surface of it, these three chapters, as the other chapters of Genesis, purport to be genuine history. Second, the Church universal has so understood these chapters up to this very time, with the exception of the dialectical theologians and their converts. Third, it is extraneous factors (geological and anthropological theories) and not biblical exegesis that have produced this deviation. Fourth, Genesis 1-3 is integrated with the rest of Genesis, which is typical history (virtually everyone admits this of Genesis 12-50, at least). Fifth, Genesis 5:1-5 specifically mentions Adam as does 1 Chronicles 1:1, in an indisputably historical sense. Sixth, the New Testament also mentions Adam in historical genealogy in Jude 14 and Luke 3:38. Seventh, Paul compares and contrasts Adam with Jesus Christ as the first and second Adam. There is a dualism here, as the demythologizers contend, but not a cosmic dualism—simply the dualism of two historical

persons in representative roles. Eighth, if Adam can be "demythologized," we see no reason to stop Bultmann from demythologizing the entire Bible, as he seems intent on doing. Ninth, if we were to demythologize, then not only can Bultmann do it to the entire Bible, but he or anyone else can interpret the demythologized Bible as he pleases.[1]

Whatever else is to be said, the claim that is made for the rest of the Bible surely applies to these chapters as well. They claim to be a revelation from God! And this is the first step toward answering the challenge, toward demonstrating that the Bible is a revelation from God—it claims to be just that.

PROJECT NUMBER 1

1. List the three ways in which the Bible claims to be a revelation from God.

2. List three verses you would use to demonstrate to the challenger the claim the Bible makes for itself.

But we can hardly expect any thinking person to be satisfied with such an answer. How could such contents ever be made known by God? We are overwhelmed by the apparently insuperable chasm between a thought in the mind of God and a thought in the mind of a human author. What means were used by God to communicate His revelation? Here is the second step toward answering our challenger.

II. The Means

The great Princeton theologian, B.B. Warfield, has suggested two classes under which the media used by God may be considered: Internal Suggestion and External Manifestation.[2] Each of these has three primary avenues.

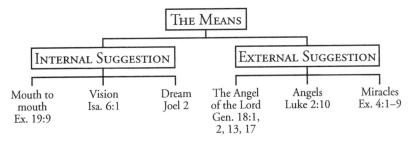

Using this wide variety of means, the Bible claims God communicated His thoughts in the minds of the human authors of Scripture.

Project Number 2

Under which of the above six avenues should each of the following references be placed?

a) Daniel 9:2 _____   d) Genesis 15:1 _____

b) 1 Kings 18 _____   e) Acts 2:22 _____

c) Daniel 2 _____   f) Hebrews 2:4 _____

But, our challenger might object, what *evidence* can we offer to support that the Bible is a revelation from God? Take a careful look at the third step. This is the most important step of all. Here is some of the very material I used that night with the ball players.

III. The Supporting Evidence

A few years ago Dr. Cyrus Hamlin of Robert College, Constantinople, was asked by a Turkish colonel to give him just one sure proof that the Bible is God's book. Dr. Hamlin asked if the colonel had ever visited the ruins of ancient Babylon. "Yes," he replied, "and let me tell you my experience. I hired a rich sheik and his men to take me there to hunt. We found that all manner of wild animals, owls, and birds were dwelling there among the ruins, so we had the best hunting of our lives. It was so good that we were annoyed when the Arabs told us they must go miles away to pitch their tents for the night. We tried to bribe them to camp right there, but they refused, saying that no Arab had ever been known to camp there, because it was haunted after dark by all manner of evil spirits." Then Dr. Hamlin opened his Bible to Isaiah 13:19-21 and the colonel read:

> And Babylon, the beauty of kingdoms, the glory of the Chaldeans' pride, will be as when God overthrew Sodom and Gomorrah. It will never be inhabited or lived in from generation to generation; Nor will the Arab pitch his tent there, nor will shepherds make their flocks lie down there. But desert creatures will lie down there. And their houses will be full of owls, ostriches also will live there, and shaggy goats will frolic there.

By this one fulfilled prophecy that Turkish colonel was convinced that the Bible is a God-inspired book. Here is the first and greatest evidence in support of the supernatural character of the Bible. It demands the verdict that the Bible is indeed what it claims to be—a revelation from God. And what is this evidence?

A. The Evidence of Fulfilled Prophecy

1. EVIDENCE FROM THE LIFE OF CHRIST

Let's chart the evidence. Here are thirty-three specific prophecies from the Old Testament referring to the birth, life, death and resurrection of Christ. These came from several different prophets, and five centuries apart (1000-500 B.C.)

	B.C.	Prophecy	Prophesied	Fulfilled
1.	487	Sold for 30 pieces of silver	Zech. 11:12	Matt. 6:14,15
2.	487	Money given to potter	Zech. 11:13	Matt. 27:5-10
3.	487	Side of Lord pierced	Zech. 12:10	John 19:34-37
4.	487	Forsaken by His disciples	Zech. 13:7	Matt. 26:56
5.	787	Darkness over the earth	Amos 8:9	Matt. 27:45
6.	1047	Christ suffered for all	Ps. 2:1,2	Luke 23:8-12
7.	1047	Christ's forsaken cry	Ps. 22:1	Matt. 27:46
8.	1047	Christ was ridiculed	Ps. 22:7	Matt. 27:41-43
9.	1047	Christ's heart broken	Ps. 22:14	John 19:34
10.	1047	His hands and feet pierced	Ps. 22:16	Luke 23:33
11.	1047	To be the seed of a woman	Gen. 3:15	Matt. 1:1
12.	712	To be born of a virgin	Isa. 7:14	Matt. 1:23
13.	4000	To be a Jew	Gen. 12:3	Matt. 1:1
14.	712	Birth to be miraculous	Isa. 9:6	Matt. 1:18-25
15.	1000	To be of the House of	David Ps. 132:11	Rom. 1:3
16.	710	To be born at Bethlehem	Mic. 5:2	Matt. 2:1-6
17.	4000	To be of the tribe of	Judah Gen. 49:10	Matt. 2:6
18.	1451	To be a prophet	Deut. 18:18	Acts 3:22
19.	606	To make a new covenant	Jer. 31:31,33	Heb. 8:7
20.	712	A light to all nations	Isa. 49:6	Luke 2:30-32
21.	487	Riding on an ass	Zech. 9:9	Matt. 21:1-7
22.	742	To be a stumbling block	Isa. 8:14 1	Cor. 1:23
23.	698	To perform miracles	Isa. 61:1,2	Matt. 11:2-6
24.	1000	Rejected by the rulers	Ps. 118:22,23	Acts 4:11
25.	758	Christ's teaching rejected	Isa. 6:9,10	Matt. 13:14
26.	600	Cleansing of the temple	Jer. 7:11	Matt. 21:13
27.	740	As a babe carried into Egypt	Hos. 11:1	Matt. 2:15
28.	1520	Promised Redeemer	Job 19:25	Gal. 4:4
29.	712	To come to His Own	Isa. 40:3	Luke 3:4
30.	712	Rejected by His Own	Isa. 53:3	John 1:11
31.	712	Christ's burial foretold	Isa. 53:9	Matt. 27:57
32.	1047	Christ's resurrection foretold	Ps. 16:10	Acts 2:24-33
33.	1047	Christ's ascension predicted	Ps. 110:1	Acts 7:55

2. EVIDENCE IN HAIFA

Some time ago *Moody* magazine drew our attention to a prophecy that was uttered sixteen centuries before Christ, the fulfillment of which transpired recently.[3] The prophecy relates to the future of Zebulun, one of the twelve tribes of Israel, and what should happen to their tribal allotment in Palestine. It was uttered by Jacob, in his blessing to the tribes, and later by Moses, as follows:

> Zebulun shall dwell at the seashore;
> And he shall be a haven for ships,
> And his flank shall be toward Sidon. (Gen. 49:13)

> And of Zebulun he said, "Rejoice, Zebulun, in your going forth,
> And, Issachar, in your tents.
> "They shall call peoples to the mountain;
> There they shall offer righteous sacrifices;
> For they shall draw out the abundance of the seas,
> And the hidden treasures of the sand." (Deut. 33:18,19)

For nearly 3,600 years since the prophecy was uttered, no port of consequence was ever built on the coast of Zebulun. But in October 1933 the British high commissioner of Palestine opened at Haifa a magnificent new harbour, which is actually under the shadow of Mount Carmel. This he did in preparation for the opening of the pipeline that has been laid to convey oil from the great oil wells of Iran 1,100 miles east.

The line is now in operation and it is declared that more than 4,000,000 tons of oil annually will be delivered to the sea at Haifa for transport. Not only has this made Zebulun increasingly "a haven of ships," but the commercial development of the land itself calls for the harbour.

The article continues to point out that Jaffa (old-time Joppa) was more suitably situated in relation to Jerusalem. But "all this was done that it might be fulfilled which was spoken by the prophet, Zebulun shall … be a haven for ships." Little did those in authority know when they built the harbour at Haifa that they were the instruments of God, fulfilling what the prophet had predicted more than 3,600 years ago. How could he have known that? Only by divine revelation.

3. EVIDENCE IN ANCIENT HISTORY

Someone has succinctly surveyed the scene:

> More than a century before Nineveh was sacked and burned by Nebuchadnezzar, while Assyria was still the greatest power in the world, and men thought it would never be overthrown, Nahum, the prophet, wrote, "She is emptied! Yes, she is desolate and waste!" (Nah. 2:10)

> While Babylon was in its prime and all the world marvelled

at its wealth and might, Jeremiah dared to foretell its doom in these striking words, "And Babylon will become a heap of ruins, … without inhabitants." (Jer. 51:37)

In the days of Tyre's supremacy in the Mediterranean, when her island fortress still proudly defied the world and her ships ruled the waves, Ezekiel dared to declare, "And they will destroy the walls of Tyre and break down her towers; and I will scrape her debris from her and make her a bare rock. She will be a place for the spreading of nets in the midst of the sea…." (Ezek. 26:4,5)

While Egypt was still a power to be reckoned with in world affairs, the same prophet announced, "It will be the lowest of the kingdoms; and it will never again lift itself up above the nations. And I shall make them so small that they will not rule over the nations." (Ezek. 29.15)

Of the beautiful temple that was standing in Jerusalem in the days of the Lord, He Himself foretold, "And He answered and said to them, 'Do you not see all these things? Truly I say to you, not one stone here shall be left upon another, which will not be torn down.'" (Matt. 24.2)

As for the city itself, He said, " … and Jerusalem will be trampled under foot by the Gentiles until the times of the Gentiles be fulfilled." (Luke 21:24)

A glance over history demonstrates how every word of these predictions has come true. The site of Nineveh is a sandy waste. All that remains of Babylon is a heap in the desert. Fishermen today spread their nets on the rocks where Tyre once stood. Certainly Egypt has never again exalted itself above the nations. As for Herod's temple, it was thrown down within forty years of the prophecy.

No wonder H.L. Hastings once wrote, "So long as Babylon is in heaps; so long as Nineveh lies empty, void, and waste; so long as Egypt is the basest of kingdoms; so long as Tyre is a place for the spreading of nets in the midst of the sea; so long as Israel is scattered among all nations; so long as Jerusalem is trodden under foot of the Gentiles; so long as the great empires of the world march on in their predicted course—so long have we proof that one Omniscient Mind dictated the predictions of that Book …"[4]

4. EVIDENCE OF CURRENT EVENTS

There are at least eight major movements before our very eyes that not only indicate the fulfillment of prophecy, but also proclaim the imminence of our

Lord's return.

First, the statehood of Israel. Daniel 9:27 assumes the existence of Israel as a state in the last days—the days of the Tribulation. The Tribulation begins with the confirming of a covenant between Israel and the Western alliance. This one prophecy assumes the existence of Israel as a state, in the land, with a covenant, aligned with the Western powers. The covenant that will be confirmed could well be the United Nations document of 1948 calling Israel into existence. If so, all that is assumed in Daniel 9:27 for the initiation of the Tribulation is true as of 1948.

Second, the alignment of the nations. In the last days there will be the king of the north (Dan. 11:15), the king of the south (Dan. 11:14), the kings of the east (Rev. 16:12) and the Western alliance of nations (Dan. 9:27). North, south, east and west in the Scriptures are always in relation to Jerusalem and Israel. These four alignments of nations around Israel are today a reality!

Third, the Western alliance of ten kings. Revelation 17:12,13 anticipates a confederacy of ten Western powers of Europe in the last days. The European Economic Community could well be the first stage of fulfillment.

Fourth, the central control of economy. This is clearly predicted of the last days in Revelation 13:17, where we are told that no man will be able to buy or sell without the mark of the beast. The decade of the '70s saw "controls" as never before.

Fifth, the abounding of lawlessness, described in Matthew 24:11.

Sixth, the profusion of war, forecast in Matthew 24:6,7.

Seventh, the threat of famine, spoken of in Matthew 24:7. Two of the greatest social problems of our day are the population explosion and the destruction of our environment. Both are major factors in the threat of famine.

Eighth, the condition of the professing church in the last days, as predicted in Revelation 17-18. According to these chapters three primary features will characterize the professing church in the last days: universality (17:1,10; 18:3), apostasy (17:3-6) and political activism (17:1,3,18). Remarkably, these are the features of the professing church today with the ecumenical movement and World Council of Churches.

Our purpose has not been to develop any of the above areas. Many others have done that in great detail recently. These are mentioned merely to point out that we are eyewitnesses to the setting of the stage for the fulfillment of myriad prophecies relating to the great drama of the last days. How could these things be known and recorded thousands of years ago? Only by revelation.

Jeanne Dixon hits about .500 by her own confession. Maurice Woodriff, who claims to have a third eye in his forehead, also engages in prophesying. Some time ago he predicted that Joe DiMaggio would remarry. When phoned, Joe denied it, but said if there was a man with a third eye he would sign him immediately to hit clean-up for his ball team!

The unerring accuracy of fulfilled prophecy witnesses to the fact that the Bible is a divine revelation.

PROJECT NUMBER 3
Research fully the details in the fulfillment of the following prophecies:

1. Tyre (Ezek. 26:4,5)
2. Destruction of Jerusalem (Luke 21:20-24)

B. The Evidence of the Unity of the Scriptures

The sixty-six books of the Bible were written over a period of 1,500 years by more than forty human writers working in three languages. They were written in many different countries by men of every degree on the social scale. Yet there is such a unity here that it is one book. Three tremendous threads tie together the pages of the Bible.

There is the thread of the Person of Christ. It is so interwoven throughout the pages of Scripture that it binds the prophecies to the fulfillments and the types to the antitypes in one beautiful mosaic of the Son of God.

There is the thread of the Plan of Redemption, which begins with the first proclamation of the gospel in Genesis 3:15 and concludes with the redeemed in eternal blessing. The uniform testimony of the Scriptures is that man's salvation is based upon the shedding of the blood of Christ in death. It is by means of God's grace and it is through faith alone.

There is also the thread of the Program of the Ages. The Bible is not a confused mass of isolated events. It records the progressive unfolding of God's plan for the ages as ordained in His eternal decree (Eph. 1:11).

There is a hidden character to the unity of the Bible. It does not lie on the surface. It is ferreted out only by diligent study and spiritual enlightenment.

More than this, there is an organic character to the unity of the Bible. The seeds are planted in the first book. They grow throughout the Bible. The culmination, the ripened fruit, is in the last book.

In giving his reasons for believing the Bible is the Word of God, R.A. Torrey suggests,

> Suppose a vast building were to be erected, the stones for which were brought from the quarries in Rutland, Vermont; Berea, Ohio; Kasota, Minnesota; and Middletown, Connecticut. Each stone was hewn into final shape in the quarry from which it was brought. These stones were of all varieties of shape and size, cubical, rectangular, cylindrical, etc., but when they were brought together every stone fitted into its place, and when put together there rose before you a temple absolutely perfect in every outline, with its domes, sidewalls, buttresses, arches, transepts—not a gap or a flaw anywhere. How would you account for it? You would say, "Back of these individual workers in the quarries was the mastermind of the architect who planned it all, and gave to each individual worker his specifications for the work."

So in the marvelous temple of God's truth which we call the Bible, those stones have been quarried at periods of time and in places so remote from one another, but where every smallest part fits each other part, we are forced to say that back of the human hands that wrought as the Master-mind that thought.[5]

PROJECT NUMBER 4

1. Trace the unity of the Scriptures in their predictions of the birth of Christ. What is prophesied in each of the following verses?
   Genesis 3:15
   Genesis 12.1-3
   Genesis 49:10
   2 Samuel 7:14
   Isaiah 7:14
   Micah 5:2
   Matthew 1:1
   Matthew 1:23
   Matthew 2:5
   Luke 1:35

2. Trace through the Scriptures one other theme of your own choice to demonstrate the unity of the Bible.

C. The Evidence of Accuracy in History and Science

Here is the third line of evidence in support of the Bible's claim to be a divine revelation. There are literally scores of examples that could be offered.

From the early nineteenth century to very recent times, the story of the invasion of Chedorlaomer and the kings of the East (Gen. 14) was viewed by critical scholars as legendary and unhistorical. Why would these invading armies ever go so far south before turning north and launching their attack on Sodom? They supposed it to be a fictional story created by Israel to honour their hero Abram. Archaeologist W.F. Albright says he once considered the extraordinary line of march that took them as far south as Kadesh before they turned northward to invade Sodom as being the best proof of the essential legendary character of the narrative. But in 1929 Albright himself discovered a line of buried cities dated at that very time along that very route. It was a well-used trade route known at that time as "The Highway of the King" (Num. 20:17). Today we know there were valuable deposits of copper, manganese, gold and other minerals in the area. There is no doubt it was this wealth that attracted the kings of the East southward. Today archaeology confirms the historical accuracy of Genesis 14.[6]

There is no doubt that archaeology has confirmed the substantial historicity of the Old Testament tradition.

Italian archaeologists working with the Israeli Department of Antiquities recently discovered in the ancient theater at

Caesarea a tablet bearing the names of Pontius Pilate and Tiberius. This is the first archaeological find to mention the Roman governor. Until this discovery our knowledge of Pontius Pilate was limited to the gospel narratives and the writings of the Jewish historian Josephus.

Dr. Abraham Biran, Director of Antiquities, stated, "Once again the veracity of the Old and New Testaments has been established."[7]

Dr. R.V.D. Magoffin, a past president of the Archaeological Institute of America, said, "Archaeology has converted both laity and clergy. No longer do they fear that archaeological investigation will overturn the Bible statements. Thus far the finds have confirmed them, or have opened confirmatory possibilities."[8]

In 1615, William Harvey discovered the circulation of the blood and that the life principle resided therein. Scientists regarded this as an amazing discovery, revealed over three hundred years ago. Says the Bible, "The life of the flesh is in the blood" (Lev. 17:11). "This is the most comprehensive and up-to-date physiological generalization that has ever been made. The life and well-being of every organ, gland, and tissue depends upon the condition and rate of the blood stream," writes a modern scientist.[9]

The truth of Leviticus 17:11 could only be known by revelation.

Isaiah 40:22 speaks of Him "who sitteth upon the circle of the earth." The word translated "circle" means an arch or a sphere. How could this have been known but by revelation?

PROJECT NUMBER 5

1. List the names of several prominent scientists who also are Bible-believing Christians.

2. Study the historical accuracy of the fall of Jericho (Josh. 6).

3. Study the scientific accuracy of Jeremiah 33:22, Leviticus 17:11, Jonah 1:17, Joshua 10:13.

Here are the three lines of supporting evidence for the Bible's claim.

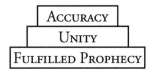

ACCURACY

UNITY

FULFILLED PROPHECY

This was the very tack I took that night with the ball players. One of them had challenged me with a question that has slain thousands and silenced tens of thousands. Frankly, I was amazed at the interest and respect these giants of the gridiron showed in the answer. Although my challenger was not convinced, he immediately became cautious. I suspect it was the first time he had even received an answer to his question.

And there is an answer. Get a handle on it before you move forward.

How do you know the Bible is true?

- It claims to be a revelation from God.
- The revelation was given through six various means.
- Its claim is supported by its prophecy, unity and accuracy.

Someone has said the Bible is not the kind of book humans would write even if they could; nor is it the kind they could write even if they would. We *would* not write such a book because it is too condemning. It categorically condemns every person as a lost and helpless sinner under the condemnation of God, and shuts us up entirely to God's grace apart from any self-righteousness and works. This is not the way we view ourselves naturally! Humans *could* not write such a book because of its unity, fulfilled prophecy and historical and scientific accuracy.

In the final analysis, however, it is as impossible to prove to any challenger that the Bible is a divine revelation from God as it is to prove the existence of God. It is the Holy Spirit who causes us to recognize Scripture as God's Word. This certainly comes from the testimony of the Spirit in our hearts. These evidences only serve to narrow the gulf that demands faith, to strengthen and confirm our faith and to demonstrate the credibility of our faith.

It was John Wesley who said that the Bible must have been written by God, good men, bad men, angels or devils. Then he observed it could not have been written by bad men or devils because of its condemnation of sin and its pronouncement of judgment. Further, he observed, it could not have been written by good men or angels because they would not deceive men by claiming God is the author. His conclusion: therefore, God must be the author.

Many will surely say Wesley's approach is rather simplistic. Although our approach has been more sophisticated, our conclusion is identical. Because of its direct claims, which are clearly substantiated by its fulfilled prophecy, unity and accuracy, we conclude that the Bible is a revelation from God.

God's thoughts were transformed, then, from His mind to the mind of the human authors of the Bible. This is the doctrine of revelation.

Think of it for a moment. That Book you hold in your hand, that Book on your bedside table, that Book on the shelf is a revelation from God! It is an unveiling of His great mind, a communication of His holy will. It is a word from God.

Art Buchwald tells about the movie epic, *The King of Kings*, the story of Jesus that was filmed several years ago in Spain. It seems that Richard Wald of the London Bureau of the *New York Herald Tribune* read a press release saying that the producer was keeping the plot a secret. He immediately asked what the release meant. The agent explained that the producer wanted it that way. "Well," said Wald, "I know a book that has the plot in it. It's called the New Testament." "For Pete's sake," pleaded the press agent, "don't tell the producer."

Can you imagine such ignorance of the Book that is a revelation from God, the Book that is the very Word of God? We cannot, we must not, we dare not ignore it.

Although we have met the challenger head on we are under no illusion. We have not yet answered his questions. Actually we have only begun. Our answer immediately triggers still another question. Any curious or contentious challenger will surely ask, But how can you be sure that what the authors recorded in their writings was an accurate record of what God had revealed to them?

After all, there is a huge gap between the revelation of something to one's mind and recording of that material in writing. This is the next gap to be bridged in the historical process. But before you proceed, a few minutes spent in review will be an investment for life.

Review

Turn back to the questions at the start of this chapter. Read them again. How many can you now answer? Surprised? I hope so. If you are still puzzled by a question go back over the chapter. Don't go on until you have mastered these questions.

FOR FURTHER STUDY

1. Examine carefully the following prophecies and their fulfillment.
   a) Micah 5:2
   b) Isaiah 44:28
   c) Daniel 9:24-27
   d) Isaiah 53
   e) Ezekiel 26:3,4,12,14; Isaiah 23:13

2. Demonstrate the supernatural unity of the Bible by tracing the following two themes throughout Scripture: redemption by blood and salvation by faith alone.

3. The historical and scientific accuracy of the Bible is seriously questioned in the account of Genesis 1-3. Isolate several of the alleged inaccuracies and answer the charges of error in each case.

END NOTES

[1] John H. Gerstner, "The Origin and Nature of Man: Imago Dei," *Basic Christian Doctrines*, Carl F. Henry (ed.), (New York, NY: Holt Rinehart and Winston, 1962), p.91.

[2] B.B. Warfield, *The Inspiration and Authority of the Bible* (Philadelphia, PA: The Presbyterian and Reformed Publishing Company, 1970), p.83.

[3] Walter B. Knight, *Three Thousand Illustrations for Christian Service* (Grand Rapids, MI: Wm. B. Eerdmans Publishing Company, 1967), p.541.

[4] Ibid, p.543.

[5] R.A. Torrey, "Ten Reasons Why I Believe the Bible is the Word of God," *Our Bible* (Chicago, IL: Moody Press, n.d.), pp.120,121.

[6] Merrill F. Unger, *Archaeology and the Old Testament* (Grand Rapids, MI: Zondervan Publishing House, 1966), p.117.

[7] Walter B. Knight, *Illustrations for Today* (Chicago, IL: Moody Press, 1970), p.25.

[8] Ibid., p.25.

[9] Walter B. Knight, *Knight's Master Book of New Illustrations* (Grand Rapids, MI: Wm. B. Eerdmans).

Part II

৯

Inspiration

CHAPTER THREE

ॐ

A SECOND ENCOUNTER

Preparing the Way

1. Define "inspiration" as it is used in the Bible.

2. How many times is the word itself used in Scripture?

3. What are the specific evidences of inspiration?

4. What was our Lord's attitude toward the Old Testament? Illustrate your answer.

5. What are some general evidences of inspiration?

6. What is so unique about the preservation of the Bible?

7. Compare and contrast the views of inspiration held by Karl Barth, C.S. Lewis, J.B. Phillips and B.B. Warfield.

8. To what extent are the Scriptures inspired?

9. Explain the verbal plenary view of inspiration.

10. What is the biblical basis for the verbal plenary view of inspiration?

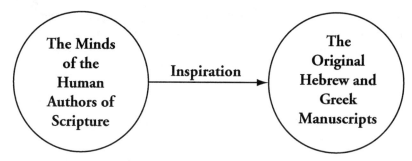

For several years now I have considered doctrinal discipleship classes to be the most significant part of my ministry. With groups of four to seven men or women, I meet weekly for an hour of fellowship in prayer and study. In these small groups I have found a quality of fellowship that has met many deep personal needs. From these groups has emerged a handful of men and women who are marked for spiritual leadership. I wish I had known enough to launch this program twenty years earlier!

The pilot group of this program was one of the most exciting foursome of men I have ever had the privilege of knowing. One was a professional football player with the Cowboys, two were in real estate, and the fourth was a partner in a growing business. Two were married, two were single. All four were relatively young Christians, extremely sharp intellectually and aggressive witnesses for Jesus Christ. It was nothing short of miraculous how God brought the group together—and kept us together.

For more than a year we met on Friday mornings from seven a.m. to nine a.m. This became the highlight of the week for each of us. Although we were different in a dozen ways, we each had a consuming desire to know the Lord, learn the Bible and serve our God. It was a period of such growth in each of our lives that we have been marked for life. We will never recover.

Facing these men for the first month was like stepping before a firing squad. These four sessions were devoted to a study of the doctrine of the Bible. We began by establishing the Bible's claim for itself—it is a revelation from God. This claim, as we now know, is well supported by the Bible's prophecy, unity and accuracy.

Then the big guns came out! Rather than solving a problem, I had actually stirred a hornet's nest. If I were to sort out their questions and simplify the issue, I think it would be stated this way: How can you be sure that what the authors recorded in their writings was an accurate record of what God had revealed to them?

That is a fair question. It also is an important one.

The answer is wrapped up in the doctrine of inspiration. This is what bridges the gap between the thoughts in the minds of the human authors and the writing of these thoughts in the original Greek and Hebrew manuscripts.

To answer the questions of my "fierce foursome" an entire session was devoted to a study of inspiration. It is the substance of that class that makes up the content of this chapter. In grappling with this subject our goal is to gain a firm grasp on the meaning of inspiration, its supporting evidence and its extent.

In probing the doctrine of inspiration in this chapter we must first establish a definition, then support it and finally consider the extent to which the Scriptures are inspired.

Today we use the word inspiration in a variety of ways. We speak of a person being "inspired" by a dynamic sermon, a moving symphony or a soul-stirring book. A select number of hymns are considered "inspirational." Certain personalities are "inspiring." Handel is said to have been "inspired" when he composed *The Messiah*. Current usage suggests some outside influence arousing within us extraordinary thoughts, feelings or actions. This is *not* the biblical meaning of inspiration.

I.   An Important Correction

In the New Testament the word occurs only once. "All Scripture is inspired by God ..." (2 Tim. 3:16) Our English phrase in the Authorized Version, "inspiration of God," was inherited from Tyndale, whose 1525 edition was the first printed English New Testament. So excellent was his work that most English versions since that time are indebted to it. However, in this case the translation is misleading and does not reflect accurately the original Greek word in 2 Timothy 3:16.

The English word "inspiration" suggests "inbreathing" or "God breathing into." The term Paul uses speaks nothing of inspiration, but only of aspiration. Literally, the Greek compound word means "God-breathed." God did not "breathe into" the Scripture nor did He "breathe into" the authors. Our text says He "breathed" the Scripture. Warfield is accurate and helpful when he says,

> In a word, what is declared by this fundamental passage is simply that all the Scriptures are a divine product, without any indication of how God has operated in producing them.[1]

First of all, it is obvious that it is the Scriptures that are inspired, not the authors. Have you ever heard someone speak of the "inspired apostle" or the "inspired writers"? Do you see the error here? It is not Paul but Paul's writings that are inspired. God so controlled the writer that what he wrote was actually "God-breathed." God breathed His Word through them.

Does this suppose that the authors were merely passive robots recording what God dictated? By no means. The individuality of each writer is seen in his peculiar style and vocabulary. In his Gospel, Luke the physician (Col. 4:14) uses a profusion of medical terms that are absent from the other three Gospels. There is a distinctive style in Paul's epistles that sets his letters apart from Peter's and John's.

Can anything be inferred concerning the accuracy of the record from the fact that it is "God-breathed"? Certainly. If it is "God-breathed" it is surely accurate and without error. Because He is the "only true God" (John 17:3), the God who cannot lie (Heb. 6:18), it is inconceivable that He should "breathe" something not true. This deduction must be examined more fully, but we shall reserve that for a later chapter. Yet it does raise a question that cannot be put off.

Isn't it impossible that an inerrant Scripture could come to us through sinful men? Not at all. As in the incarnation of the living Word, Jesus Christ, so in the inspiration of the written Word, the Bible, there is a unique blending of the human and divine. In the incarnation the Son of God came into the world through Mary, but was a "holy thing" (Luke 1:35) wholly untainted by the sinful nature of His mother. As He who is absolutely holy, pure and perfect came through one who was unholy, fallen and imperfect, so the Word of God, which is holy and true, came through fallen and sinful men.

Although in both cases the channels were imperfect, in the providence of God the products were unaffected.

It hardly needs to be mentioned that inspiration applies only to the recording of God's revelation in the original manuscripts. This is obvious.

Now put these pieces together in your definition of inspiration. In substance it will conform to that of Dr. C.C. Ryrie who says,

> Biblical inspiration may be defined as God's superintending human authors so that, using their own individual personalities, they composed and recorded without error His revelation to man in the words of the original autographs.[2]

From B. B. Warfield came a similar definition when he said, "Inspiration is the supernatural influence exerted on the sacred writers by the Spirit of God, by virtue of which their writings are given Divine trustworthiness."[3]

Project Number 1

1. List the essential points that must be included in any definition of inspiration.

2. What is the basis for such a doctrine? What does it rest on?

II. More Evidences

The evidences in support of the biblical doctrine of inspiration fall into two classifications: specific and general.

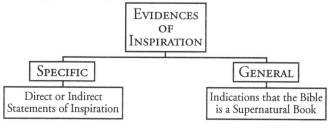

A. The Specific Evidences

Many direct and indirect statements in the Bible regarding its inspiration may be marshalled as specific supporting evidence. As an aid to memory it will be helpful to organize them into four classes.

1. THE TESTIMONY OF PAUL

> All Scripture is inspired by God and profitable for teaching,
> for reproof, for correction, for training in righteousness. (2
> Tim. 3:16)

This is the primary and central text on inspiration. It makes three major contributions to our subject.

It specifies the value of Scripture. It is useful for teaching doctrine, for reproving false teachers, for correcting those misled by heresy and for instructing the people of God in a righteous walk. It is "all" useful. Have you ever wondered about the profit of those chapters of genealogies or those lists of kings?

Mr. Newman, an agnostic, once challenged J.N. Darby on this very point. He quoted, "When you come, bring the cloak which I left in Troas with Carpus, and the books, especially the parchments" (2 Tim. 4:13). Then he asked, "What relevance is there in this verse?" At the time Darby was living frugally in Ireland as a missionary and told Newman it was this very verse that had kept him from selling his small library when he went out to Ireland as a missionary. You can count on it. Everything God says in His Word is profitable!

More than that, it declares the ultimate origin of "all Scripture." It is God-breathed! That which is the product of God is described here as "Scripture." This phrase includes all the books of the Old Testament canon, which were by that time gathered into an authoritative corpus of literature. It is to this collection that Paul refers when he speaks in verse 15 of the "Holy Scriptures" that Timothy had been taught from childhood. The word "Scripture" is a technical term for authoritative divine writings. It also occurred "currently in Philo and Josephus to designate that body of authoritative books which constituted the Jewish 'Law'."[4]

The "Scripture" of verse 16 includes not only the books of the Old Testament, but also those of the New Testament, some of which were still unwritten! The word Paul uses for "Scripture" had become a technical word for the New Testament books too. Paul uses it in 1 Timothy 5:18, where he refers to an Old Testament quotation from Deuteronomy 25:4 and a New Testament quotation from Matthew 10:10 as "Scripture." Peter refers to Paul's letters as "Scripture" in 2 Peter 3:16. In 2 Timothy 3:16, Paul does not define the limits of "Scripture" but asserts that everything that is "Scripture" is God-breathed.

The third contribution of our text is by way of implication. When he says all Scripture is God-breathed, Paul implies something about the nature of Scripture. It is divine, true and authoritative.

2. The testimony of Peter

> But know this first of all, that no prophecy of Scripture is a
> matter of one's own interpretation, for no prophecy was ever
> made by an act of human will, but men moved by the Holy
> Spirit spoke from God. (2 Pet. 1:20,21)

This coincides exactly with the testimony of Paul. Peter is particularly
occupied with one segment of Scripture—the prophetic Scriptures. However,
what is true of them is true of all Scriptures. What is that? Peter gives it nega-
tively, then positively.

It was not "by an act of human will." The Scriptures did not originate
with humans! In the entire context Peter is speaking of authentication, not
interpretation, and here states that the authors did not make up what they
wrote. This is the truth conveyed in the Authorized Version's troublesome
phrase of verse 20, "no prophecy of Scripture is of any private interpretation."
That is, it did not originate with the prophet himself, nor is it the product of
his own investigation.[5]

Positively, it came as "men moved by the Holy Spirit spoke from God."
Here the human and divine elements in inspiration are again affirmed. "Men
spoke." These were the human authors. But they did not speak on their own
initiative, of their own thoughts, for their own purposes. Calvin says, "They
did not blab their inventions of their own accord or according to their own
judgments." They spoke as they were "moved by the Holy Spirit." Peter uses
an intriguing metaphor here. The Greek verb translated "moved" is used in
Acts 27:15,17 where a ship is "carried along" by the wind. Submissive to the
Holy Spirit then, these holy men of old were "carried along," "borne along,"
in the direction He wished to take them.

In one sense this text coincides exactly with the testimony of Paul. It
asserts the divine origin of the Scriptures. It emphatically denies any human
origin. However, in another sense it actually goes further than Paul's testimony.

Peter includes the human element. "Men spoke; God spoke. Any proper
doctrine of Scripture will not neglect either part of this truth."[6] The major
contribution of this text is in its explanation of how men recorded the truth of
God's revelation. They were moved, borne along, carried along. It is in this
phrase that we see the superintending work of God in inspiration. It also identifies the specific, divine agent of inspiration to be the Holy Spirit.

3. The testimony of Christ

Our Lord believed the entire Old Testament was inspired. He said,

> Do not think that I came to abolish the Law or the Prophets;
> I did not come to abolish, but to fulfill. For truly I say to you,
> until heaven and earth pass away, not the smallest letter or
> stroke shall pass away from the Law, until all is accomplished.
> (Matt. 5:17,18)

That would be so only if all the books of the law were inspired of God. Also, He explicitly testified that David was speaking by the Holy Spirit when Christ said:

> He said to them, "Then how does David in the Spirit call
> Him 'Lord' …?" (Matt. 22:43)

In John 10:35 He bore testimony to the divine nature of the Old Testament when He said, "the Scripture cannot be broken." Further witness from our Lord can be seen in Matthew 12:3,5; 19:4 and Mark 12:24.

4. THE TESTIMONY OF OTHERS

Scores of witnesses could be called to the stand here. Let me mention only a few. David claims it for himself in 2 Samuel 23:1 (cf. Mark 12:36). Nehemiah recognizes that the prophets spoke by the Holy Spirit (Neh. 9:3,30) and that the law given by Moses was God's law (Neh. 10:29). Luke says it was the Holy Spirit who was speaking through Isaiah (Acts 28:25). Paul virtually claims inspiration for himself when he says, "the things I write unto you are the commandments of the Lord" (1 Cor. 14:37). Again, Paul considered Luke's Gospel to be "Scripture" and places it on equal footing with the Old Testament Scripture (1 Tim. 5:18, Luke 10:7). Peter designates Paul's epistles as "Scripture" also (2 Pet. 3:16).

PROJECT NUMBER 2

Complete the following chart on the specific evidence of inspiration.

This multitude of direct and indirect statements constitutes the specific supporting evidences for the inspiration of the Bible. But there is also an impressive array of general evidences.

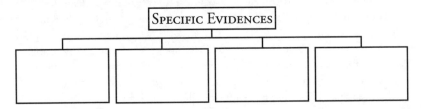

SPECIFIC EVIDENCES

B. The General Evidences

All indications apart from specific statements that the Bible is a supernatural book constitute the general supporting evidences of inspiration.

Of course, inspiration cannot be proved. As it is impossible to prove the existence of God, so it is impossible to prove the inspiration of Scripture. Obviously it claims to be inspired. The myriad direct and indirect statements establish that point. But anyone can make such claims. What evidence is there in support of this claim?

In the previous chapter we considered three evidences of revelation: ful-filled prophecy, the unity of the Bible, and its historical and scientific accuracy. These point to the supernatural original of the Bible and therefore indicate the superintending work of God and the Holy Spirit in inspiration as well.

But that is not all. There are indications from three other major areas that this is a supernatural book, inspired by God. These are the general evidences.

1. THE TESTIMONY OF HISTORY

From the pages of human history come statements of philosophers, scholars, students, theologians, politicians, artists and historians to the effect that this is a unique and supernatural book. From its unique and supernatural nature, we can infer its authority.

Josephus, the unbelieving Jewish historian of the first century, spoke of his people's attitude toward the Bible when he said,

> How firmly we have given credit to these books of our own nation is evident in what we do; for during so many ages as have already passed no one hath been so bold as either to add anything to them, to take anything from them, or to make any change; but it is become natural to all Jews, immediate-ly and from their very birth, to esteem these books to contain divine doctrine, and to persist in them, and if occasion be, willing to die for them.[7]

Robert E. Lee, American soldier and educator said, "The Bible is a book in comparison with which all others in my eyes are of minor importance, and which in all my perplexities and distresses has never failed to give me light and strength."

William E. Gladstone, prime minister of England, said, "The Bible is stamped with specialty of origin and an immeasurable distance separates it from all competitors."

Mathematician and philosopher Sir Isaac Newton said, "We account the Scriptures of God to be the most sublime philosophy. There are more sure marks of authority in the Bible than in any secular history whatever."

"The Bible is the best book in the world," said John Adams, second presi-dent of the United States.

The American orator and statesman Daniel Webster once prophesied, "If we abide by the principles taught in the Bible, our country will go on prosper-ing; but if we in our prosperity neglect its instruction and authority, no man can tell how sudden a catastrophe may overwhelm us and bury all our glory in profound obscurity."

Sir Walter Scott, when he was dying, asked his friend Lockhart to read to him. Looking over the 20,000 books in his costly library, Lockhart asked, "Which book would you like?" "Need you ask," said Scott, "There is but One."

The testimony of history from every age and every field is that this is a supernatural book.

2. THE TESTIMONY OF ITS INFLUENCE

John Richard Green begins his second volume of *A Short History of the English People* with these words:

> No greater moral change ever passed over a nation than passed over England during the years which parted the middle of the reign of Elizabeth from the meeting of the Long Parliament. England became the people of the book, and that Book was the Bible.

Under the influence of the Bible, women have been liberated from their status of inferiority, hospitals have been erected for the care of the sick, a reverence for human life has developed, the significance of marriage and the role of the partners has been revolutionized, and the institution of slavery has collapsed.

J.B. Phillips, well-known translator of the Bible, shares this thrilling story:

> Some years before the publication of the New English Bible, I was invited by the BBC to discuss the problems of translation with Dr. E.V. Rieu, who had himself recently produced a translation of the four Gospels for Penguin Classics. Towards the end of the discussion Dr. Rieu was asked about his general approach to the task, and his reply was this: "My personal reason for doing this was my own intense desire to satisfy myself as to the authenticity and the spiritual content of the Gospels. And, if I received any new light by an intensive study of the Greek originals, to pass it on to others. I approached them in the same spirit as I would have approached them had they been presented to me as recently discovered Greek manuscripts."

> A few minutes later I asked him, "Did you get the feeling that the whole material is extraordinarily alive? … I got the feeling that the whole thing was alive even while one was translating. Even though one did a dozen versions of a particular passage, it was still living. Did you get that feeling?"

> Dr. Rieu replied, "I got the deepest feeling that I possibly could have expected. It changed me; my work changed me. And I came to the conclusion that these words bear the seal of the Son of Man and God. And they're the Magna Carta of the human spirit."

> I found it particularly thrilling to hear a man who is a scholar of the first rank as well as a man of wisdom and experience openly admitting that these words written long ago were alive with power. They bore to him, as to me, the ring of truth.[8]

When an atheist challenged H.A. Ironside to debate the existence of God, he accepted on one condition. The atheist was to bring ten men with him who would testify as to how their lives had been enriched by the teaching of atheism and Ironside would bring one hundred. The atheist never did show up.

Dr. A.T. Pierson wrote in the nineteenth century:

> The Bible is the greatest traveller in the world. It penetrates to every country in the world, civilized and uncivilized. It is seen in the royal palace and in the humble cottage. It is the friend of emperors and beggars. It is read by the light of the dim candle and amid Arctic snows. It is read in the glare of the equatorial sun. It is read in city and country, amid the crowds and in solitude. Wherever its message is received it frees the mind from bondage and fills the heart with gladness.[9]

The influence of the Scriptures supports the claim that it is God-breathed.

3. THE TESTIMONY OF ITS PRESERVATION

In tribute to the indestructibleness of the Bible, A.Z. Conrad has written:

> Century follows century—there it stands.
> Empires rise and fall and are forgotten—there it stands.
> Dynasty succeeds dynasty—there it stands.
> Kings are crowned and uncrowned—there it stands.
> Despised and torn to pieces—there it stands.
> Storms of hate swirl about it—there it stands.
> Atheists rail against it—there it stands.
> Profane, prayerless punsters caricature it—there it stands.
> Unbelief abandons it—there it stands.
> Thunderbolts of wrath smite it—there it stands.
> The flames are kindled about it—there it stands.
> The arrows of hate are discharged against it—there it stands.
> Fogs of sophistry conceal it temporarily—there it stands.
> Infidels predict its abandonment—there it stands.
> The tooth of time gnaws but makes no dent—there it stands.
> An anvil that has broken a million hammers—there it stands. [10]

In spite of the passing of time, the Bible still stands. We used to say that one out of every twenty books will last seven years. Now it is probably less than that. School textbooks are quickly outdated. What book 500 years old is read by masses of common people?

In spite of the persecution of its enemies, the Bible still stands.

Voltaire said that in a hundred years the Bible would not be read. One hundred years later a press was printing Bibles in his very home in France. Thomas Paine once said, "In five years from now there will not be a Bible in

America. I have gone through the Bible with an axe and cut down all the trees." Today it still stands.

Dr. Torrey writes:

> This book has always been hated. No sooner was it given to the world than it met the hatred of men, and they tried to stamp it out. Celsus tried it by the brilliancy of his genius; Porphyry by the depth of his philosophy, but they failed. Lucian directed against it the shafts of his ridicule; Diocletian the power of the Roman Empire, but they failed. Edicts backed by all the power of the empire were issued that every Bible should be burned, and that everyone who had a Bible should be put to death. For eighteen centuries every engine of destruction that human science, philosophy, wit, reasoning or brutality could bring to bear against that book to stamp it out of the world has been used, but it has a mightier hold on the world today than ever before.[11]

Someone has said the Bible is like the Englishman's wall that was built three feet high and four feet wide. When asked why, he said, "I built it that way so that if the storms should come and blow it over, it will be higher afterwards than before." The Bible stands higher today than ever!

"After forty-five years of scholarly research in biblical textual studies and language study," said the late Robert Dick Wilson, Ph.D., professor of Semitic Philology at Princeton Theological Seminary, "I have come now to the conviction that no man knows enough to assail the truthfulness of the Old Testament. Wherever there is sufficient documentary evidence to make an investigation, the statements of the Bible, in the original text, have stood the test."[12]

PROJECT NUMBER 3

1. Complete the following chart on the general evidences in support of the inspiration of the Bible.

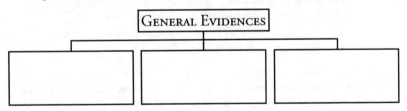

2. Discuss the assertion that "Many books influence life. Only the Bible transforms life."

In a survey reported in *Christianity Today* (Sept. 11, 1970), the question was asked, "Do you believe the Bible is the inspired Word of God?" This question received a negative answer from 87 percent of Methodists who responded, 88 percent of Presbyterians, 95 percent of Episcopalians, 67 percent of American Baptists and 77 percent of American Lutherans. Karl Barth is clear and precise in rejecting the orthodox doctrine of inspiration, which he calls "the lame hypothesis of the 17th Century doctrine of inspiration."[13]

And yet there are six major evidences that have been brought forward in defence of its claims that the Bible is a supernatural book. They are:

- fulfilled prophecy
- the unity of the Scriptures
- the historical and scientific accuracy
- the testimony of history
- the astounding influence of the Bible
- its amazing preservation

Every Christian should memorize these six evidences and be prepared to illustrate each one. Although they are not conclusive, they cannot be ignored! There is extensive evidence to support the claim of inspiration.

Yet, it is one thing to acknowledge that the Bible is a book inspired by God, but quite another thing to say all the Bible, every part of the Bible, is God-breathed.

We may be prepared to admit the first, but the second—that causes many to choke just a little. Here is a fair question, To what extent are the Scriptures actually inspired of God?

III. A Matter of Controversy

There are several schools of thought even among evangelicals on the extent of inspiration.

A. The Varying Degree View of Inspiration

Some, for example, believe there are varying degrees of inspiration in the Bible. Who better to represent this school than C.S. Lewis, who wrote: "All Holy Scripture is in some sense—though not all parts of it in the same sense—the word of God.[14]

He explained what he meant when he said:

> Something originally merely natural—the kind of myth that is found among most nations—will have been raised by God above itself, qualified by Him and compelled by Him to serve purposes which of itself it would not have served.[15]

Obviously, then, although he has a high view of the text, Lewis sees varying degrees of inspiration, especially in the Old Testament Scriptures.

It is this view that may say the story of the flood was originally of Mesopotamia, but was elevated by God above itself and incorporated into the Bible to teach a lesson.

B. The Conceptual View of Inspiration

Others maintain that only the concepts of the Bible are inspired. J.B. Phillips speaks for this school when he says: "Any man who has sense as well as faith is bound to conclude that it is the truths which are inspired and not the words, which are merely the vehicles of truth."[16]

He rejects any idea that the actual words of Scripture are inspired. Only the ideas or concepts transmitted to the minds of the authors are considered as God-breathed.

However there is a fatal weakness here. Concepts must be communicated through words. There is no other way. For God's concepts to be communicated to the authors and for these men to communicate those thoughts to us, words had to be used. For that concept to be conveyed accurately the words must be inspired. Otherwise there is no guarantee that the thought has been precisely expressed.

C. The Partial View of Inspiration

It is increasingly popular today to say that the trustworthiness of the Scriptures applies only to matters of faith and doctrine, not history—in matters of salvation, Scripture is inspired; in matters of history or science, it is not. That is, inspiration is restricted to those parts of Scripture that are doctrinal.

But 2 Timothy 3:16 says, "All Scripture is God-breathed." Not part of it, but *all* of it. Furthermore, the line between doctrine and history can be very subjective and arbitrary. Who can draw such a line? Where is it to be drawn in Genesis 3?

D. The Verbal Plenary View of Inspiration

It seems difficult to avoid the fact of the verbal plenary inspiration of Scripture. Verbal inspiration is the inspiration of the words themselves (not the ideas or truths) in the original. Paul rests his argument of Galatians 3:16 upon a doctrine of verbal inspiration. Here the difference between a singular ("seed") and plural ("seeds") in Genesis 12:7; 13:15; and 17:7 is the basis of Paul's argument. The very letters of a word are reliable, therefore inspired.

Does not Matthew 5:18 imply that our Lord believed in verbal inspiration? In speaking of the sacred writings of the Jews, the Old Testament, He says:

> For truly I say to you, until heaven and earth pass away, not
> the smallest letter or stroke shall pass away from the Law,
> until all is accomplished.

The "jot" of the Authorized Version is the smallest letter of the Hebrew alphabet—*yodh* ('). It is similar to our apostrophe. Probably the "tittle" is the very small horn on the Hebrew letter *daleth* (ד) which distinguishes it from the letter *resh* (ר). Speaking on this verse, R. Laird Harris observes: "He says very positively that this Book is perfect to smallest detail. It is not merely verbal inspiration that teaches here, but inspiration of the very letter!"[17]

In the parallel passage, Luke 16:17, our Lord says, "But it is easier for heaven and earth to pass away than for one stroke of a letter of the Law to fail."

Note also the Lord's comment about His own words in Luke 21:33: "Heaven and earth will pass away, but My words will not pass away.

In Matthew 22:43, the Lord's entire argument revolves around the single word "My." David spoke of Messiah as "*My* Lord" (emphasis added). That was a confession to His deity. Observe especially that the "my" in the original Hebrew text was one letter only—a *yodh*. This is an amazing corroboration of Matthew 5:18. His entire defence of His deity rests upon the reliability of one letter, the smallest of all Hebrew letters.

The main objection to verbal inspiration is that it leads to a very wooden view of the Bible. Some say it destroys the humanity of the authors if they passively recorded, as secretaries, what God dictated. Obviously a dictation view of inspiration is untenable. The styles and vocabularies of the writers differ greatly according to their background and training. They certainly were not passively recording what was being dictated to them.

But verbal inspiration does not require a dictation view. It was achieved by the Holy Spirit who superintended the human authors as they chose words from their vocabulary.

Philosophically, verbal inspiration is a logical necessity because the only way to accurately communicate concepts or truths is by words. As this is God's purpose in revelation and inspiration, it demands His direct personal involvement in the words used. Our Lord testifies to this. The apostles assume it.

The correct view of inspiration includes not only verbal but also plenary inspiration. Plenary inspiration speaks of the inspiration of the entire Bible, of every word in the Bible, not just certain parts. There are no degrees of inspiration. "All Scripture is God-breathed" (2 Tim. 3:16).

Clark Pinnock expresses it well when he says,

> Inspiration guarantees all that Scripture teaches. It is a seamless garment, an indivisible body. Jesus Christ accepted no dichotomy or dualism in Scripture between true and false, revealed and unrevealed matters. His attitude was one of total trust. For example, He obviously regarded the entire Old Testament history as factually correct; the Gospels record at least twenty allusions to incidents from the creation of Adam to Daniel's prophecies and Jonah's preaching. He regarded the entire Scripture as trustworthy, the commonplace as well as the extraordinary.[18]

The same author quotes from a sermon delivered in 1858, by J.C. Ryle on 2 Corinthians 2:17. Ryle said,

> We corrupt the Word of God most dangerously, when we throw any doubt on the plenary inspiration of any part of Holy Scripture. This is not merely corrupting the bucket of living water, which we profess to be presenting to our people, but poisoning the whole well. Once wrong on this point, the whole substance of our religion is in danger. It is a flaw in the foundation. It is a worm at the root of our theology. Once allow the worm to gnaw the root, and we must not be surprised if the branches, the leaves, and the fruit, little by little, decay.

> The whole subject of inspiration, I am aware, is surrounded with difficulty. All I would say is, notwithstanding some difficulties which we may not be able now to solve, the only safe and tenable ground to maintain is this—that every chapter, and every verse, and every word in the Bible has been given by inspiration of God. We should never desert a great principle in theology any more than in science, because of apparent difficulties which we are not able at present to remove.[19]

As "verbal" stands against the conceptual view of inspiration, so "plenary" stands against the partial and varying degree views of inspiration. What is the extent of inspiration? It extends to the very words and to *all* the words.

PROJECT NUMBER 4

1. Why is the doctrine of inspiration important?
2. What, then, is your answer for my four friends who want to know how we can be sure the Bible contains an accurate record of God's revelation to man?

A notable New Testament scholar was once approached by an ardent admirer pouring forth his praise. To the scholar he said, "I've always wanted to meet a theologian who stands on the Word of God."

Quietly the reply came back, "Thank you sir, but I do not stand on the Word of God, I stand under it."

Where else is there to stand if, indeed, it is the revealed inspired Word of God? Do you stand under it in your creed and conduct, your faith and practice?

R. Laird Harris sounds a solemn warning when he says,

> In Bunyan's *Pilgrim's Progress,* we read that at one point in his journey Pilgrim slept awhile and lost his scroll. Bunyan grippingly pictures the anxiety and trouble that ensued until

Pilgrim retraced his steps and found his book. America has lost its belief in and emphasis upon the Bible. There was a time when it was read and taught in our schools. Now more than the most perfunctory reading of it is said to be illegal. It used to be preached, memorized, quoted, studied and believed. Now this is true only in restricted circles. America must return to the Bible. But we shall not return to the Bible as long as it is regarded merely as great literature. It is only when we receive it as God's holy and infallible Word that it will bring the promised blessing.[20]

We have now bridged two gigantic gaps in the historical process. The gap from God's mind to the authors' minds is spanned by revelation, and the gap from the authors' minds to the original writings is spanned by inspiration.

These two tremendous truths carry with them two implications of the greatest possible magnitude. One implication set off a very heated controversy (battle!) a few years ago. The other is calculated to shatter many a dream and revolutionize every life. It is to these very implications that we turn in the following two chapters.

Review

Before you move on to chapter four take time to review. It is never time wasted. It will yield rich dividends as you proceed. Turn back to those ten questions that stumped you at the beginning of the chapter. How many can you answer now?

When you have control of the answers for all ten, you are ready for chapter four.

For Further Study

1. Trace the history of verbal inspiration through the history of the church.

2. Critique fully the opposing views of inspiration: varying degrees, partial, conceptual and dictation.

3. In what sense can you say a part of the Scriptures is inspired which was copied by the author from some literature outside the Bible (e.g., Titus 1:12)?

End Notes

[1] B.B. Warfield, *The Inspiration and Authority of the Bible* (Philadelphia, PA: The Presbyterian and Reformed Publishing Company, 1970), p.133.

[2] C.C. Ryrie, *The Holy Spirit* (Chicago, IL: Moody Press, 1967), p.33.

[3] B.B. Warfield, *The Inspiration and Authority of the Bible*, p.133.

[4] Ibid., p.133.

[5] M. Green, *The Second Epistle of Peter and the Epistle of Jude* (Grand Rapids, MI: Wm. B. Eerdmans Publishing Company, 1968), p.90.

[6] Ibid., p.91.

[7] Flavius Josephus, "Against Apion" I, 8. *The Works of Flavius Josephus*, Trans. by Wm. Whiston (London, Wm. P. Nimm), p.609.

[8] J.B Phillips, *The Ring of Truth* (New York, NY: The MacMillan Company, 1967), pp.74,75.

[9] Quoted by A. Naismith, *The Veracity and Infallibility of the Bible* (Grand Rapids, MI: Gospel Folio Press, n.d.), p.5.

[10] Quoted by Walter B. Knight, *Knight's Illustrations for Today* (Chicago, IL: Moody Press, 1970), p.22.

[11] R.A. Torrey, "Ten Reasons Why I Believe the Bible Is the Word of God," *Our Bible* (Chicago, IL: Moody Press, n.d.), p.123.

[12] Quoted by Walter B. Knight, *Knight's Illustrations for Today* (Chicago, IL: Moody Press, 1970), p.22.

[13] Karl Barth, *Church Dogmatics*, G.W. Bromiley and T.F. Torrance (eds.), (Edinburgh, 1936-62), III, Part 1, p.24.

[14] C.S. Lewis, *Reflections on the Psalms* (New York, NY: Harcourt, Brace and World, Inc., 1958), p.19.

[15] Ibid., p.111.

[16] J.B. Phillips, *The Ring of Truth*, pp.21,22.

[17] R. Laird Harris, *Inspiration and Canonicity of the Bible* (Grand Rapids, MI: Zondervan Publishing House, 1969), p.46.

[18] Clark Pinnock, *Biblical Revelation* (Chicago, IL: Moody Press, 1971), p.87.

[19] Ibid., p.88.

[20] R. Laird Harris, *Inspiration and Canonicity of the Bible*, pp.70,71.

Bibliography

Harris, R. Laird. *Inspiration and Canonicity of the Bible*. Grand Rapids, MI: Zondervan Publishing House, 1957.

Pinnock, Clark. *Biblical Revelation*. Chicago, IL: Moody Press, 1971.

Ryrie, Charles Caldwell. *The Holy Spirit*. Chicago, IL: Moody Press, 1965.

Warfield, Benjamin Breckinridge. *The Inspiration and Authority of the Bible*. Philadelphia, PA: The Presbyterian and Reformed Publishing Company, 1970.

Young, Edward J. *Thy Word Is Truth*. Grand Rapids, MI: Wm. B. Eerdmans Publishing Company, 1967.

Part III

આ

INERRANCY

CHAPTER FOUR

&

COMPLETELY TRUSTWORTHY

Preparing the Way

1. What is the meaning of "inerrancy"?

2. Distinguish between inerrancy and infallibility.

3. Does the Bible claim inerrancy for itself? If so, how and where?

4. What arguments can be marshalled in defence of inerrancy?

5. Is inerrancy an important doctrine? Why or why not?

6. Is inerrancy a recent phenomenon? Did the early church fathers believe it?

7. Regarding the current debate over inerrancy, four positions can be distinguished among evangelicals. What are they?

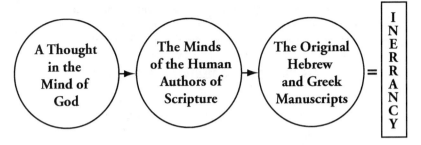

Recently I read of a seminary student who was serving as student pastor of a small church. Expressing the concern of his congregation he asked, "My people ask me, 'If the Bible says it, can I believe it?'"[1]

That's a fair question! It is also a common and critical question. Our answer, "It is completely trustworthy." That is what we mean by "inerrancy."

Few subjects are more divisive.

Some people blatantly deny inerrancy. An accepted authority among spiritualists, Dr. Moses Hull, once wrote these outrageous words:

> The Bible is, I think, one of the best of the sacred books of the ages. It is supposedly the sacred fountain from which two, if not three, of the greatest religions of the world have flowed... . While the Bible is not the infallible or immaculate book that many have supposed it to be, no one can deny that it is a great book... . Yet it must be confessed that the age of critical analysis of all its sayings and its environments has hardly dawned... . John R. Shannon said to his Denver audience, "We do not believe in the verbal inspiration of the Bible. The dogma that every word of the Bible is supernaturally dictated is false. It ought to be shelved away... . Verbal inspiration is a superstitious theory; it has turned multitudes in disgust from the Bible; it has led thousands into infidelity; it has led to savage theological warfare... . All these facts would show if brought out, that the Bible, like all other books, is exceedingly human in its origin. While the Bible is, none of it infallible, none of it unerring—when rightly interpreted it is, all of it, useful, all of it good."[2]

Others quietly ignore it. One large denomination in North America recently chopped the word "inerrant" from its statement of faith. For years many of our most influential evangelical leaders have refused to deny it openly. Rather they have quietly chosen to refuse to affirm it.

"To those in the broader theological community, this seems an irrelevant issue, a carry-over from an antiquarian view of the Bible."[3]

To many evangelicals, however, it is extremely important. The argument takes the form of a logical conclusion.

Granted that God did reveal Himself to the human authors and that the human authors, under the influence of the Holy Spirit, did record accurately what was revealed to them, what are the implications for the Scriptures?

Revelation + Inspiration = Inerrancy

If the Bible is a divine revelation that has been God-breathed then, they say, the inerrancy of the Scriptures naturally follows. This is what is to be explored in this chapter.

Inerrancy means different things to different people. Consider, for example, the various evangelical theories on inerrancy as summarized by H. Wayne House in the following chart.

Evangelical Theories on Inerrancy [4]		
Position	**Proponent**	**Statement of Viewpoint**
Complete Inerrancy	Harold Lindsell Roger Nicole Millard Erickson	The Bible is fully true in all its teaches or affirms. This extends to the areas of both history and science. It does not hold that the Bible has a primary purpose to present exact information concerning history and science. Therefore the use of popular expressions, approximations and phenomenal language is acknowledged and believed to fulfill the requirement of truthfulness. Apparent discrepancies, therefore, can and must be harmonized.
Limited Inerrancy	Daniel Fuller Stephen Davis William LaSor	The Bible is inerrant only in its salvific doctrinal teachings. The Bible is not intended to teach science or history, nor did God reveal matters of history or science to the writers. In these areas the Bible reflects the understanding of its culture and may therefore contain errors.
Inerrancy of Purpose	Jack Rogers James Orr	The Bible is without error in accomplishing its primary purpose of bringing people into personal fellowship with Christ. The Scriptures, therefore, are truthful (inerrant) only in that they accomplish their primary purpose, not by being factual or accurate in what they assert. (This view is similar to the Irrelevancy of Inerrancy view.)

Evangelical Theories on Inerrancy [4] (continued)		
Position	**Proponent**	**Statement of Viewpoint**
The Irrelevancy of Inerrancy	David Hubbard	Inerrancy is essentially irrelevant for a variety of reasons: (1) Inerrancy is a negative concept. Our view of Scripture should be positive. (2) Inerrancy is an unbiblical concept. (3) Error in the Scriptures is a spiritual or moral matter, not an intellectual one. (4) Inerrancy focuses our attention on minutiae, rather than on the primary concerns of Scripture. (5) Inerrancy hinders honest evaluation of the Scriptures. (6) Inerrancy creates disunity in the church. (This view is similar to the Inerrancy of Purpose view.)

Complete inerrancy declares the Scriptures to be completely trustworthy in all they affirm. There is total agreement among advocates of this position in terms of their view of the theological or spiritual message. They may, however, differ in their understanding of the scientific and historical references. In contrast to Lindsell, for example, Nicole regards scientific and historical elements as phenomenal.[5] That is,

> [T]hey are reported as they appear to the human eye. They are not necessarily exact; rather they are popular descriptions, often involving general references or approximations. Yet they are correct. What they teach is essentially correct in the way they teach it.[6]

I. A Closer Look

What then do we mean when we speak of the inerrancy of Scripture? We mean it is completely truthful and trustworthy in all of its teachings. Though the expressions may vary, the essence is consistent in a multitude of popular and current statements.

James Cottrell, writing on the inerrancy of the Bible, says,

> It means "without error, mistake, contradiction or falsehood." It means "true, reliable, trustworthy, accurate, infallible." To say that the Bible is inerrant means that it is absolutely true and trustworthy in everything that it asserts; it is totally without error.[7]

Dr. Charles C. Ryrie makes a helpful distinction when he writes,

> Inerrant means "exempt from error" and dictionaries consider
> it a synonym for infallible which means "not liable to deceive,
> certain." Actually there is little difference in the meaning of the
> two words, although in the history of their use in relation to
> the Bible, "inerrant" is of much more recent use.[8]

By many today, infallibility is used in reference to faith and morals, while inerrancy is used in reference to the entire text of the Scriptures.

In spite of its problems, inerrancy is a word that captures the essence of the reliability of Scripture. James Boice quotes Paul Feinberg, who gave us a careful and expanded definition when he wrote,

> Inerrancy means that when all the facts are known, the
> Scriptures in their original autographs and properly interpret-
> ed will be shown to be wholly true in everything they teach,
> whether that teaching has to do with doctrine, history, sci-
> ence, geography, geology or other disciplines or knowledge.[9]

Pause for a moment to consider the importance of the above phrase "properly interpreted." This is a crucial factor in the doctrine of inerrancy. Authors obviously used common and accepted figures of speech as poetic languages (i.e., the mountains singing), phenomenal language (i.e., the sun standing still), and the rounding off of numbers. More than that, they apparently rearranged chronology to suit their purpose or interest. This is quite evident in the Gospels. These and a dozen other elements must be incorporated into a "proper interpretation of Scripture" and allowed within the scope of inerrancy.

At the Chicago summit meeting of the International Council on Biblical Inerrancy in October, 1978, several hundred key evangelical leaders signed this statement:

> Being wholly and verbally God-given, Scripture is without
> error or fault in all its teaching, no less in what it states about
> God's acts in creation and the events of world history, and
> about its own literary origins under God, than in its witness
> to God's saving grace in individual lives.[10]

The Lausanne Covenant addressing the authority and power of the Bible declares, "We affirm the divine inspiration, truthfulness and authority of both Old and New Testament Scriptures in infallible rule of faith and practice."

The doctrinal basis of the Evangelical Theological Society states, "The Bible alone, and the Bible in its entirety, is the Word of God written and is therefore inerrant in the autographs."

The World Evangelical Fellowship affirms "[t]he Holy Scriptures as originally given by God, divinely inspired, infallible, entirely trustworthy; and the supreme authority in all matters of faith and conduct."

The doctrine on inerrancy, then, asserts four things:

- The Scriptures are without error. They are wholly true.
- This applies to the original writings of the authors.
- They are without error in everything:
  - doctrine and ethics;
  - history and science.
- They are wholly true in all they affirm or teach.

II. The Defence

The arguments in support of the doctrine of inerrancy generally fall into four broad categories: inferential, deductive, inductive and historical.

A. The Inferential Argument

This has been expressed in the terms of the equation

Revelation + Inspiration = Inerrancy

The inference of inerrancy is inescapable. If it is inspired, it is inerrant. If it is God-breathed, it is trustworthy. Pope Leo XIII recognized this when he wrote:

> For all the books … are written wholly and entirely, with all their parts, at the dictation of the Holy Spirit, and so far is it from being possible that any error can coexist with inspiration, that inspiration not only is essentially incompatible with error, but excludes and rejects it as it is impossible that God Himself, the Supreme Truth can utter that which is not true.[11]

Although he was incorrect in describing inspiration as "the dictation of the Holy Spirit," he was surely correct in his inference that error cannot coexist with inspiration.

But the claim of inerrancy is based upon more than inference.

B. The Deductive Argument

A deduction is a process of reasoning from the general to the specific. The general in this case is the character of God. What kind of God is the God of the Bible? Observe the common characteristic in these select verses.

> May it never be! Rather, let God be found true, though every man be found a liar, as it is written, "THAT THOU MIGHTEST BE JUSTIFIED IN THY WORDS, AND MIGHTEST PREVAIL WHEN THOU ART JUDGED." (Rom. 3:4)

> And this is eternal life, that they may know Thee, the only true God, and Jesus Christ whom Thou has sent. (John 17:3)

> In order that by two unchangeable things, in which it is impossible for God to lie, we may have strong encouragement, we who have fled for refuge in laying hold of the hope set before us. (Heb. 6:18)

> God is not a man, that He should lie, nor a son of man, that He should repent; has He said, and will He not do it? Or has He spoken, and will He not make it good? (Num. 23:19)

If God is true, the word He breathes must also be true. If He cannot lie, the Word of God must be inerrant.

The argument for inerrancy is actually in the form of a syllogism. By its very nature, the conclusion of a syllogism is of necessity true if the two premises are true. Here is a typical example:

> All men are mortal (major premise).
> Caesar is a man (minor premise).
> Therefore Caesar is a mortal (necessary conclusion).

In the argument for inerrancy the syllogism is as follows:

> Major Premise: Every Word of God is true—inerrant (Titus 1:2, Heb. 6:18).
> Minor Premise: The Bible is God's Word (direct assertions: Matt. 15:6, Rom. 9:6, Ps. 119:105, Rom. 3:2, Heb. 5:12; inference: 2 Tim. 3:16).

Speaking about 2 Timothy 3:16, B.B. Warfield helpfully observes:

> The Greek term has ... nothing to say of inspiring: it speaks only of a "spiring" or "spiration!" What it says of Scripture is not that it is "breathed into by God," or that it is the product of the divine "in-breathing" into its human authors, but that it is breathed out by God.... When Paul declares, then, that "every Scripture," or "all Scripture," is the product of the divine breath, "is God-breathed," he asserts with as much energy as he could employ that Scripture is the product of a specifically divine operation.[12]

Conclusion: The Bible is inerrant, truth, without lie.

This is the necessary conclusion. It can be denied only by denying one or both of the premises.

The Bible then, makes two basic claims: it asserts unequivocally that God cannot lie, and that the Bible is the Word of God. It is primarily from a combination of these two facts that the doctrine of inerrancy comes.

The character of God requires it.

Of course, the weakness of such a deduction is transparent. The premise—the character of God—is based upon the teaching of the Bible. It is virtually a circular argument using verses from the Bible to attest to the truthful character of God, from which we deduce the Bible is trustworthy. The strength of any deduction rests in the truthfulness of the premise. If one is prepared to accept the truthfulness of God (whether or not it is based upon biblical texts) then there is some validity to this deduction. Otherwise it is not a conclusive argument. However, inerrancy does not depend upon a deduction. There is still a much more forceful line of argument.

C. The Inductive Argument

An induction is the process of reasoning from many specifics to a general conclusion. There is a host of particular phrases in the Scriptures that may be accumulated and lead to the conclusion that the Scriptures are inerrant.

PROJECT NUMBER 1

Consider the following verses carefully. What specific point is made in each verse that makes this verse part of the inductive process that leads to inerrancy?

John 10:35

Matthew 5:17-18

Galatians 3:16

2 Timothy 3:16

Isaiah 45:19

Proverbs 30:5,6

Jeremiah 1:9

1 Corinthians 2:13

The confidence of Christ, the apostles and the prophets in the Scriptures argue for their total accuracy. Put together these specifics, and the general conclusion surely is that the Scriptures are inerrant.

D. The Historical Argument

Those denying inerrancy often claim that this doctrine is a recent invention. Some say it originated with Princeton theologian B.B. Warfield in the late 1880s. Others, such as Jack Rogers of Fuller Theological Seminary, trace it back to the Lutheran theologian Turretin, just after the Reformation.

Both views are wrong. Inerrancy was taught long before Calvin and Luther. Augustine said:

> I have learned to yield this respect and honor only to the canonical books of Scripture. Of these alone do I most firm- ly believe that the authors were completely free from error.[13]

St. Thomas Aquinas, the great medieval theologian wrote, "Nothing false can underlie the literal sense of Scripture" (Summa Theologica I, 1, 10, ad 3). Martin Luther repeated over and over, "The Scriptures have never erred," and "The Scriptures cannot err."[14]

Erickson clarifies a critical point when he writes,

> While there has not been a fully enunciated theory until modern times, nonetheless there was, down through the years of the history of the church, a general belief in the complete dependability of the Bible. Whether this belief entailed precisely what contemporary inerrantists mean by the term "inerrancy" is not immediately apparent. Whatever the case, we do know that the general idea of inerrancy is not a recent development.[15]

Obviously, the idea of inerrancy was not a late invention of the post-Reformation period or of the nineteenth century American theologians. It was the belief of the early church fathers and the great Reformers. It was the belief of Clement, Irenaeus and Justin Martyr, as well as Calvin and Luther.

III. What About Limited Inerrancy?

A distinct but prestigious minority of evangelical scholars strongly opposes strict inerrancy as defined above. They do not believe the Bible is inerrant in all it affirms.

They advocate a limited or partial inerrancy. According to such scholars, the Scriptures are inerrant only in revelational matters: faith and practice or doctrine and ethics. When it speaks on the deity of Christ, the salvation of man, the nature of sin or the sovereignty of God, it is entirely trustworthy.

However, such men deny the inerrancy of Scripture in matters of science and history. When it records genealogies, creation data or historical events it is not entirely trustworthy. They maintain that the critical phenomena of the Bible discredit inerrancy, for all it affirms.

For my part, the Bible does not seem to distinguish between doctrinal and historical matters. As a matter of fact, often, it is very difficult to separate the doctrine from the history (e.g., Matt. 19:4)[16] If inerrancy does not extend to all that the Scriptures affirm, how can we really speak of inerrancy?

PROJECT NUMBER 2

1.   What further biblical illustrations can you offer to demonstrate there is no way to seperate the doctrine from the historical event?

2.   How do you account for the drift from inerrancy in evangelicalism today?

PROJECT NUMBER 3

Discuss the validity and implications of this statement: "Inerrancy is fundamental—but it is not a fundamental of the faith."

   That is, it is fundamental and important to the issue of authority. It does reflect upon the character of God. It is an essential part of the foundation of a dynamic and mature Christian life. But it is not in the same category as the great fundamentals—the virgin birth, the deity of Christ, the substitutionary death of Christ, etc. And because it is not "a fundamental," it should not be an issue over which fellowship with other Christians is broken.

   While "militant advocates" of strict inerrancy are united in their defence of absolute inerrancy, they are divided over the priority of the doctrine. They believe inerrancy is a doctrinal watershed that one must hold to be considered evangelical. It is a fundamental doctrine, the denial of which is grounds for the severance of fellowship (e.g., Harold Lindsell).

   The "peaceful advocates" believe that inerrancy is not specifically taught in Scripture and therefore is not a priority issue, not a doctrinal watershed (e.g., Carl F. H. Henry).

IV. Does Inerrancy Really Matter?

Not every evangelical believes that inerrancy really matters. Some say inspiration matters, but not inerrancy. Or they say, what is really important is a personal relationship with Jesus Christ.

   For several reasons, inerrancy does matter.

   To deny the inerrancy of Scripture seems to be inconsistent with true discipleship to Christ. Our Lord Jesus taught that Scripture was true right down to the smallest part (Matt. 5:18). Elsewhere He declared, "The Scripture cannot be broken" (John 10:35). Inerrancy is important as long as Jesus is Lord, and to all who claim Him as Lord.

   On this point, Boice helpfully writes:

> A person's relationship to Jesus Christ is of the highest importance. No Christian would ever want to dispute that. But how do you know Jesus except as He is presented to you in the Bible? If the Bible is not God's Word and does not present a picture of Jesus Christ that can be trusted, how do you know it is the true Christ you are following? You may be worshiping a Christ of your own imagination. Moreover, you

have this problem. A relationship to Jesus is not merely a question of believing on Him as one's Savior. He is also your Lord, and this means He is the one who is to instruct you as to how you should live and what you should believe. How can He do that apart from an inerrant Scripture? If you sit in judgment on Scripture, Jesus is not really exercising His Lordship in your life. He is merely giving advice which you consider yourself free to disobey, believe or judge in error. You are actually the lord of your own life.[17]

To deny inerrancy is to undermine the authority of Scripture. Can one really embrace as "an infallible rule of faith and practice" a book one believes to contain errors, discrepancies and contradictions? Although some today profess to do so, their position is untenable. Biblical inerrancy is inseparably linked to the larger question of biblical authority. Evangelicals who deny inerrancy must show how they distinguish the truths from the errors of the Bible without, in the process, making themselves the final authority on what they will accept and reject. G. Aiken Taylor, while asking, Is God as good as His Word? writes,

> The person who allows doubts about the reliability of Scripture to linger or to be nourished, will soon discover that his confidence in the authority of Scripture is shaken. Finally, his effectiveness in the use of Scripture will diminish.[18]

B.B. Warfield correctly observed: "The authority which cannot assure of a hard fact is soon not trusted for a hard doctrine."[19]

To deny inerrancy is to open the door to other errors that will creep into the church and corrupt it doctrinally. Norman Geisler observes that Harold Lindsell has shown, in his *Battle For The Bible*,

> … example after example of schools and institutions which began their descent into modernism by a denial of the inerrancy of Scripture. He concluded, therefore, that inerrancy is a "watershed" issue. All things being equal, once this fundamental doctrine of Scripture is denied, there is a serious crack in the dam and sooner or later there will be a collapse. That is to say, once someone cannot trust the Bible when it speaks of history or science, then his confidence is eroded on other matters, even those pertaining to salvation.[20]

PROJECT NUMBER 4
Does inerrancy really matter? How important is it really? What other arguments can you add to the three listed above?

Beware!

James Boice sounds an alarm that ought to awaken and arouse every evangelical alive today when he writes,

> For the last hundred years Christians have seen the Bible attacked directly by modern liberal scholarship and have recognized the danger. Today a greater danger threatens—the danger of an indirect attack in which the Bible is confessed to be the Word of God, the only proper rule for Christian faith and practice, but is said to contain errors.
>
> This threat is greatest because it is often unnoticed by normal Christian people. If a liberal denies the virgin birth, questions the miracles of Christ or even declares that Jesus was only a man (as many are still doing), most Christians recognize this for what it is—unbelief. They see the hand of Satan in it. He is the one who questioned the Word of God in the first recorded conversation in the Bible, "Did God really say, 'You must not eat from any tree in the garden?' ... You will not surely die ... God knows that when you eat of it your eyes will be opened, and you will be like God, knowing good and evil" (Genesis 3:1,4). But if someone pretending to be an evangelical says, "Sure I believe in the Bible as you do, but what difference does it make if there are a few mistakes in it? After all, the Bible isn't a history book. It's not a science book. It only tells us about God and salvation." Many Christians fail to see that this is also an attack on the Bible and so have their faith undermined without their even knowing it.[21]

Review

Once again you will find it most worthwhile to take a few minutes to review the material of this chapter. Turn back to the questions under "Preparing The Way" at the start of this chapter, and be sure you are able to answer each one completely and correctly.

FOR FURTHER STUDY

In view of the inerrancy of Scripture, how can the following problems be resolved?

1. The problem of the missing thousand: 1 Corinthians 10:8, Numbers 25:9.

2. The synoptic problem:
   a) e.g., Matthew 22:42 and Luke 20:41—What did He say?

b) e.g., Luke 24:4 and Matthew 28:2—How many angels were there?

3. The problem of Abiathar: Mark 2:26 and I Samuel 21:1 ff.—Who was the high priest?

4. The problem of the mustard seed: Matthew 13:31,32—Is it indeed the smallest seed?

END NOTES

[1] Millard J. Erickson, *Introducing Christian Doctrine* (Grand Rapids, MI: Baker Book House, 1992), p.62.

[2] Victor H. Ernest, *I Talked with Spirits* (Wheaton, IL: Tyndale House Publishers, 1972), pp.41,42.

[3] Millard J. Erickson, *Introducing Christian Doctrine*, p.60.

[4] H. Wayne House, *Charts of Christian Theology and Doctrine* (Grand Rapids, MI: Zondervan Publishing House, 1992), p.24.

[5] Harold Lindsell, *The Battle for the Bible* (Grand Rapids, MI: Zondervan Publishing House, 1976), pp.165,166. Roger Nicole, "The Nature of Inerrancy," *Inerrancy and Common Sense*, Roger Nicole and J. Ramsey Michaels (ed.), (Grand Rapids, MI: Baker Book House, 1980), pp.71-95.

[6] Millard J. Erickson, *Introducing Christian Doctrine* (Grand Rapids, MI: Baker Book House, 1992), p.61.

[7] Jack Cottrell, "*The Inerrancy of the Bible*," The Evangelical Recorder, (March, 1979), p.12.

[8] Charles C. Ryrie, *The Bible: Truth without Error*, revised edition (Dallas Theological Seminary, 1977), p.1.

[9] James Montgomery Boice, *Does Inerrancy Matter?* (International Council on Biblical Inerrancy, 1979), p.13.

[10] "The Short Statement of the International Council on Biblical Inerrancy," Statement No. 4. Published in *Christianity Today*, (November 17, 1978), p.36.

[11] Papal Encyclical 3292 in Heinrick Demzinger, *Sources of Catholic Dogma*.

[12] Quoted by James Montgomery Boice, *Does Inerrancy Matter?* p.15.

[13] Augustine, *Letters*, LXXXII.

[14] Martin Luther, *Works of Luther XV*: 1481; XIX: 1073.

[15] Millard J. Erickson, *Introducing Christian Doctrine*, p.62.

[16] For further reading see Norman L. Geisler, "The Inerrancy Debate—What Is It All About?" *Interest* (November, 1978), p.5.

[17] James Montgomery Boice, *Does Inerrancy Matter?* pp.24-25.

[18] G. Aiken Taylor, "Is God As Good As His Word?" *Christianity Today* (February 4, 1977), p.24.

[19] B.B. Warfield, *The Inspiration and Authority of The Bible* (Philadelphia, PA: The Presbyterian and Reformed Publishing Company, 1970), p.442.

[20] Norman L. Geisler, "The Inerrancy Debate—What Is It All About?" *Interest* (November, 1978), p.3

[21] James Montgomery Boice, *Does Inerrancy Matter?* p.28.

BIBLIOGRAPHY

Beagle, Dewey M. *The Inspiration of Scripture*. Philadelphia, PA: Westminster Press, 1963.

— *Scripture Tradition and Infallibility*. Grand Rapids, MI: Wm. B. Eerdmans, 1973.

Bloesch, Donald G. *Holy Scripture*. Downers Grove, IL: InterVarsity Press, 1994.

Boice, James Montgomery (ed.). *The Foundation of Biblical Authority*. Grand Rapids, MI: Zondervan Publishing House, 1978.

Boice, James Montgomery. *Does Inerrancy Matter?* International Council on Biblical Inerrancy, 1979.

Cottrell, Jack. "The Inerrancy of the Bible." *The Evangelical Recorder*, March, 1979.

Davis, Stephen T. *The Debate about the Bible*. Philadelphia, PA: Westminster Press, 1977.

Dowey, Edward A., Jr. *The Knowledge of God in Calvin's Theology*. New York, NY: Columbia, 1952.

Erickson, Millard J. *Introducing Christian Doctrine*. Grand Rapids, MI: Baker Book House, 1992.

Geisler, Norman L. "The Inerrancy Debate—What Is It All About?" *Interest*, November, 1978.

Lindsell, Harold. *The Battle for the Bible*. Grand Rapids, MI: Zondervan Publishing House, 1976.

— *The Bible in the Balance*. Grand Rapids, MI: Zondervan Publishing House, 1980.

Montgomery, John Warwick (ed.). *God's Inerrant Word*. Minneapolis, MN: Bethany Fellowship, 1974.

Mounce, Robert R. "Clues to Understanding Biblical Inaccuracy." *Eternity*, June, 1966.

Pache, Rene. *The Inspiration and Authority of Scripture*. Chicago, IL: Moody Press, 1969.

Packer, J.I. *"Fundamentalism" and the Word of God*. Grand Rapids, MI: Wm. B. Eerdmans, 1958.

Pinnock, Clark H. *A Defense of Biblical Infallibility*. Philadelphia, PA: Presbyterian and Reformed Publishing Company, 1967.

Radmacher, Earl D. (ed.). *Can We Trust The Bible?* Wheaton, IL: Tyndale House, 1979.

Rogers, Jack (ed.). *Biblical Authority*. Waco, TX: Word, 1977.

Ryrie, Charles C. *What You Should Know About Inerrancy*, Revised 1977. Chicago, IL: Moody Press, 1981.

Schaeffer, Francis A. *No Final Conflict*. Downers Grove, IL: InterVarsity Press, 1976.

Stahr, James. "Are There Errors In The Bible?" *Interest*, March, 1978.

— James. "Round 2—The Battle For The Bible." *Interest*, September, 1979.

Stott, John. *The Authority of the Bible*. Downers Grove, IL: InterVarsity Press, 1974.

Taylor, G. Aiken. "Is God As Good As His Word?" *Christianity Today*, February 4, 1979.

Warfield, B.B. *The Inspiration and Authority of the Bible*. Philadelphia, PA: The Presbyterian and Reformed Publishing Company, 1970.

Part IV

ॐ

AUTHORITY

CHAPTER FIVE

ॐ

A DESPERATE DILEMMA

Preparing the Way

1. Why is the matter of authority such a problem for the Christian Church? Does it really matter what your authority is?

2. The question of authority has divided Christendom into two major divisions today. What are they?

3. What are the four major contemporary criteria for authority?

4. What evidence is there that the Scriptures are the final authority?

5. How can the Bible be said to be authoritative when there are different interpretations of the Bible?

6. Is the Bible the only authority of the Christian? Is it the Bible interpreted by reason or by experience that is authoritative, or is it neither?

7. What is the witness of the Spirit and how does it relate to the question of authority?

8. Why is there such a weak attitude today toward the authority of the Scriptures?

9. What is the scope of the Bible's authority?

10. What are the implications of the authority of the Scripture for the movement for church unity, the lifestyle of the Christian and the condition for salvation?

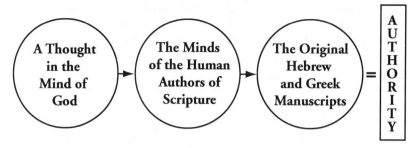

"Karen" was one of the loveliest young ladies I have ever met. Although I had heard a great deal about her, our first personal encounter took place in my study several years ago. She had phoned and asked to see me about a personal problem. An hour or two later she appeared at my door—with a girl friend. To my surprise both were carrying Bibles.

I listened as she told me of her recent conversion to Christ. What an amazing story that was. God had invaded her neat and comfortable life. For several years she had lived life to the full. She had tasted the pleasures this old world has to offer and enjoyed them all. Then came her new birth. She was born again into the family of God. She had committed her life to Jesus Christ.

Now she was in a dilemma. Although she was unmarried, she was living with a man who also had recently become a Christian. They loved one another and needed one another.

Her parents were horrified. Her Christian friends were critical. Yet her boyfriend refused to consider a change in their relationship. In the midst of it all she was being torn to pieces.

For almost an hour we sparred. I used every argument I knew, and there are many, in my attempt to persuade her to abandon a lifestyle that was destroying her. It almost seemed, however, that the more I tried to convince her of the error of her way, the more convinced she became of its rightness.

Eventually, about an hour too late, I finally saw the problem at the root of her dilemma. It is one of the most basic and important issues in every life. It is the question of authority.

Every area of every life is touched by this issue. Every struggle is a confrontation with the question of authority. To resolve this conflict is to settle a thousand storms that will rage in every believer's bosom. It is to this end that our present chapter is dedicated.

The concept of authority is not a popular one today. The world of Woodstock rejects it. The militant revolutionary attacks it. The women's liberation movement redefines it. The draft dodger defies it. Parents and civil authorities surrender it. And yet, the real question is not, Authority or not authority? but rather What is the authority? Each one has an authority. This

dictates the direction of life and determines one's principles. This is at the root
of the dilemma my young friend faced in my office that afternoon. "Karen's"
problem was really one of authority. This is no new problem.

I. A Perennial Problem

It is certainly no overstatement to say, "The problem of authority is the most
fundamental problem that the Christian Church ever faces."[1]

This is no exaggeration. Any survey of church history will attest to its
truthfulness. But why? Why is the issue of authority so central? There are
three major reasons.

A. The nature of the message

In contrast to many world religions, which are based upon ideas and princi-
ples, Christianity is built upon objective revealed truth. Its message is, "But
God demonstrates His own love toward us in that while we were yet sinners,
Christ died for us" (Rom. 5:8).

The promise is eternal life:

> And the witness is this, that God has given us eternal life, and
> this life is in His Son. He who has the Son has the life; he
> who does not have the Son of God does not have the life.
> These things I have written to you who believe in the name
> of the Son of God, in order that you may know that you have
> eternal life. (1 John 5:11-13)

It commands us to trust Jesus Christ personally for our salvation. It is a
message to be obeyed and promises the judgment of God for those who disobey (John 3:36, 1 Pet. 4:17, 2 Thess. 1:8). It asserts that Jesus Christ,
through His substitutionary death, is the only way of salvation (John 14:6,
Acts 4:12). The central message of the Christian gospel is the uniqueness of
Jesus as the only way to God. There is salvation in none other.

Obviously, the exclusiveness of the Bible's message invites a challenge to
its authority. The authority behind such a message is absolutely basic. It is of
critical significance.

B. The search for truth

What is truth? The question of Greek philosophers, echoed by Pilate, has been
asked by millions down through the centuries. Is there any truth? Where is it?
What is the criterion of truth? When a Christian steps forward to answer these
questions, one finds oneself immediately embroiled in the controversy over
authority.

C. The threat to the unity of the church

In the days of the apostle Paul, cracks began to appear in the building of God—the church. The deepest and most serious could be traced to the problem of authority. In Ephesus, Timothy was cautioned against accepting as an authority the profane babblings of the Gnostics (1 Tim. 6:20,21), which threatened the unity of the church.

The question of authority still divides Christians today. James I. Packer says:

> It is the most far-reaching and fundamental division that there is, or can be, between them. The deep cleavages in Christendom are doctrinal; and the deepest doctrinal cleavages are those which result from disagreement about authority. Radical divergences are only to be expected when there is no agreement as to the proper grounds for believing anything.[2]

Doctrinal divisions within Christendom may be sorted into two general classifications according to their basis of authority, suggests Packer.[3]

Many with doctrinal differences actually work from the same basic authority—that is, the Word of God. Arminians and Calvinists differ in their theology, yet both acknowledge the Scriptures to be their sole authority. So also Baptist and Presbyterians or amillennialists and premillennialists.

These agree that there is one authority only—the Scriptures. However, they disagree on what the Scriptures teach. This raises an interesting question. How can the Scriptures be considered as authoritative when they are subject to various interpretations? For the moment, this question will have to be put on the shelf.

There is a second major classification within Christendom however. This class includes the wide variety of groups that rest their case upon different authorities.

For the traditionalist, the authority is tradition; for the existentialist, the authority is personal experience. The rationalist's authority is reason. The evangelical's authority is the Bible.

Hence, Protestants and Roman Catholics differ in their theology because they differ in their authorities. So also, liberals and evangelicals, existentialists and orthodox believers.

Outside Christian thought there are the heathen, the atheist, the agnostic and others. These differ with one another as well as with other groups because they differ in their authorities.

Here, then, are the three major reasons why the problem of authority is the most fundamental problem we face: the Christian's message, the world's search and the church's destiny.

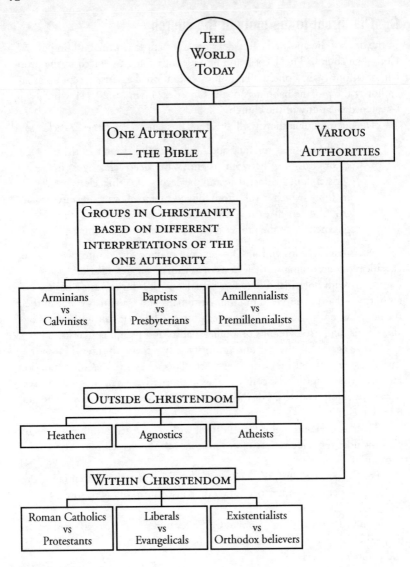

PROJECT NUMBER 1

Using the chart above as a guide, place these names in the appropriate places on the following chart.

Billy Graham   Francis Schaeffer
Guru Maharaji ji   New Age Movement
Thomas Paine   Hare Krishna
Transcendental Meditation   Charles Colson
Corrie Ten Boom   Mohammed Ali

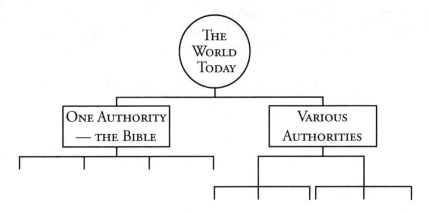

The problem we faced in my study that afternoon was no new problem. In my corner I had said, "No! Stop! Change!" In the other corner Karen had said, "Why? I can't! I don't want to!" In another corner of her mind stood her parents, her church and her Christian friends. Opposite them stood her boyfriend and her society. What a dilemma!

II. The Real Question

Although she felt sure the question was whether to leave or not to leave, that was not the real question. For an hour we sparred, with little progress because I failed to see the root problem. As soon as it was exposed I asked, "Karen, what is the authority for your conduct as a Christian?"

That is it! What is your standard for measuring truth, for marking right and wrong? What is your criterion? What is the ultimate authority for your faith and conduct? This is the real question I pressed upon the conscience and life of my friend that afternoon. There are four popular standards on the scene today. I was not sure where to categorize Karen. I knew, however, that her next words would do that for me. It would put her in one of the following four folds.

A. The Rule of Reason

This is the criterion of the rationalist. In a rationalist the intellect reigns supreme. The premise is this: If it is reasonable, it is true! If it is not reasonable, I cannot accept it.

The rationalist's basic assumption is that the mind in its processes is capable of discovering, organizing and stating truth. Actually there are two categories of rationalists as they relate to the Word of God.

1. REASON *without* THE SCRIPTURES

Some such persons totally reject the Scriptures as revelation. These are the atheists, the agnostics, the skeptics and the infidels. To Thomas Paine, Ingersoll and Voltaire, revelation and reason were mutually exclusive.

After writing some fine pamphlets on freedom, including *The Rights of Man*, Thomas Paine wrote *The Age of Reason* and said it would destroy the Bible. He claimed that within one hundred years Bibles would be found only in museums or in musty corners of second-hand bookstores.

Ingersoll held up a copy of the Bible and said, "In fifteen years I'll have this book in the morgue." Fifteen years rolled by and Ingersoll was in the morgue, but the Bible lives on.

Voltaire's reason rejected the Scriptures also. He predicted that in one hundred years the Bible would be an outmoded and forgotten book. When the one hundred years had passed, Voltaire's house was owned and used by the Geneva Bible Society. And note this. Recently ninety-two volumes of Voltaire's works—a part of the Earl of Derby's library—were sold for two dollars.

2. REASON *above* THE SCRIPTURES

Others recognize the Bible as literature of worth, but place their reason above the Scriptures. These are the theological liberals. Packer suggests that such a person accounts for the Bible this way:

> Scripture is certainly a product of outstanding religious insight. God was with its authors. They were inspired to write, and what they wrote is inspiring to read. But their inspiration was not of such a kind as to guarantee the full truth of their writings, or to make them all the Word of God. Like all human products, Scripture is uneven. One part contradicts another; some parts are uninspired and unimportant; some of it reflects an antiquated outlook which can have no relevance for today. (The same, of course, on this view is true of church tradition). If the essential biblical message is to mean anything to modern man, it must be divorced from its obsolete trappings, reformulated in the light of modern knowledge and restated in terms drawn from the thought-world of today. Reason and conscience must judge Scripture and tradition, picking out the wheat from the chaff and refashioning the whole to bring it into line with the accepted philosophy of the time.[4]

But is reason really adequate? Pascal, the French philosopher and mathematician, pointed out that the supreme function of reason is to show us that some things are beyond reason. And surely they are.

Reason as the ultimate authority is not an authentic Christian position. The darkness of the human mind prevents it from being such.

> But a natural man does not accept the things of the Spirit of God; for they are foolishness to him, and he cannot understand them, because they are spiritually appraised. (1 Cor.2:14)

> In whose case the god of this world has blinded the minds of the unbelieving that they might not see the light of the gospel of the glory of Christ, who is the image of God. (2 Cor. 4:4)

> This I say therefore, and affirm together with the Lord; that you walk no longer just as the Gentiles also walk, in the futility of their mind, being darkened in their understanding, excluded from the life of God, because of the ignorance that is in them, because of the hardness of their heart. (Eph. 4:17,18)

One of the most staggering statements in Scripture relative to this subject comes from the pen of Paul. He writes, "There is none who understands" (Rom. 3:11). The verb the Holy Spirit uses here occurs twenty-six times in our New Testament but is reserved for a peculiar use. It is invariably used for understanding divine things. Our Lord uses it for understanding the things of the kingdom (Matt. 13:13,14,15,19,23,51). Paul speaks of understanding what the will of the Lord is (Eph. 5:17).

Although people think they understand, and they talk and write extensively on the subject, yet humanity, by nature, understands nothing about God or truth!

George Whitefield, a master preacher, once was depicting a blind man with his dog, walking on the brink of a precipice. His foot was almost slipping over the edge. The description was so graphic, the illustration so vivid and life-like, that Lord Chesterfield sprang up and exclaimed, "Good God! He's gone!"

But Whitefield answered, "No, my lord, he is not quite gone; let us hope that he may yet be saved." Then he went on to speak of the blind man as a man being led by his reason. What a graphic way of showing that a man led only by reason is ready to fall into hell!

If reason is not a legitimate authority, what is? For centuries a mainstream within Christendom has proposed a second standard—tradition.

B. The Test of Tradition

This is the criterion of the traditionalist, who is frequently found in Roman Catholicism, the Orthodox tradition and some Protestant churches. For the traditionalist, the official teaching of the institutional church is the rule for life and faith.

The premise, stated simply, is this: "To learn the mind of God one should consult the church's historic tradition; what the church says, God says."[5]

The basic assumption is that the Bible is not a sufficient and complete revelation. Packer again is very helpful here.

> This view does not question that the Bible is God-given and therefore authoritative; but it insists that Scripture is neither sufficient nor perspicuous, neither self-contained nor self-interpreting, as an account of God's revelation. The Bible alone, therefore, is no safe nor adequate guide for anyone. However, tradition, which is also God-given and therefore authoritative, supplies what is lacking in Scripture; it augments its contents and declares its (alleged) meaning.[6]

Rome paved the way in this direction and has gone furthest down the road. It was the Council of Trent in 1546 that declared tradition of equal authority with the Bible. It stated that the Word of God is contained both in the Bible and in tradition and urged every Christian to give them equal veneration. The Vatican Council of 1870 proclaimed infallibility of the pope in matters of faith and morals.

While rationalism and modernism take away from the Word of God, this position adds to it. The position of the Roman Catholic church is clearly and succinctly stated by Loraine Boettner who writes:

> She maintains that alongside of the written Word there is an oral tradition, which was taught by Christ and the apostles but which is not in the Bible, which rather was handed down generation after generation by word of mouth. This unwritten Word of God, it is said, comes to expression in the pronouncements of the church councils and the papal decrees. It takes precedence over the written Word and interprets it. The pope, as God's personal representative on the earth, can legislate for things additional to the Bible as new situations arise.[7]

Devoted followers in this church are required to make this confession:

> I also admit the holy Scriptures, according to that sense which our holy mother Church has held and does hold, to which it belongs to judge of the true sense of interpretation of the Scriptures; neither will I ever take and interpret them otherwise than according to the unanimous consent of the Fathers.[8]

But is this a legitimate Christian stance? Hardly, for several reasons. Let me mention briefly only three.

There is, first of all, the unreliability of oral tradition. The disputed doctrines are without any biblical validation or any support from the writings of the fathers in the second and third centuries. Therefore, for hundreds of years that which is allegedly tradition was passed on orally. Can such material be placed on equal authority with the written Scriptures? If it was revealed truth, why is there no written record of it earlier? If it was merely reported repeatedly from one generation to the next for several generations, what guarantee is there of its genuineness?

Also, the contradictions in early tradition make it suspect. Boettner graphically demonstrates this point when he writes:

> The church Fathers repeatedly contradict one another. When a Roman Catholic priest is ordained, he solemnly vows to interpret the Scriptures only according to "the unanimous consent of the Fathers." But such "unanimous consent" is purely myth. The fact is they scarcely agree on any doctrine. They contradict each other, and even contradict themselves as they change their minds and affirm what they previously had denied. Augustine, the greatest of the Fathers, in his later life wrote a special book in which he set forth his Retractions. Some of the Fathers of the second century held that Christ would return shortly and that He would reign personally in Jerusalem for a thousand years. But two of the best known scholars of the early church, Origen (185-254), and Augustine (354-430), wrote against this view. The early Fathers condemned the use of images in worship, while later ones approved such use. The early Fathers almost unanimously advocated the reading and free use of the Scriptures, while the later ones restricted such reading and use. Gregory the Great, bishop of Rome and the greatest of the early bishops, denounced the assumption of the title of Universal Bishop as anti-Christian. But later popes, even to the present day have been very insistent on using that and similar titles which assert universal authority. Where, then, is the universal tradition and unanimous consent of the Fathers to papal doctrine?[9]

Finally, the oral tradition does not complete, but rather nullifies the Scriptures. Consider the most prominent doctrines and practices of this church, their distinctives if you like, and compare them to Scripture: the papacy (cf. Matt. 22), the priesthood (cf. 1 Pet. 2:5,9), the celibacy of the priests and nuns (cf. Gen. 2:18), the use of images in worship (cf. Ex. 20:4,5), worship of the Virgin Mary (cf. Matt. 4:10), penance and indulgences (cf. Eph. 2:8,9), prayers for the dead (cf. Heb. 9:27), the mass (cf. Heb. 9:28) and purgatory (cf. Luke 16:23).

Each of these and a host of others are founded solely on tradition and appear to oppose the teachings of Scripture.

It is indeed difficult to resist the conclusion of Boettner who says:

> We insist, however, that it would have been utterly impossible for those traditions to have been handed down with accuracy generation after generation by word of mouth and in an

atmosphere dark with superstition and immorality such as
characterized the entire church, laity and priesthood alike,
through long periods of its history. And we assert that there
is no proof whatever that they were so transmitted. Clearly
the bulk of those traditions originated with the monks during the Middle Ages.[10]

One of the most remarkable trends in the religious world today is the
breaking up of this foundation. Many adherents to such churches are saying
that final authority does not really lie in the church, but ultimately in the conscience of men. This brings us to the third criterion.

Although a remnant still hold to them, the rule of reason and the test of
tradition are largely past. Our generation has witnessed the rise of a "new cult
of madness." In it "reason" and "logic" are dirty words. Thinking is repudiat-
ed. Age-old petrified planks of tradition are trampled under foot. A new sovereign has been crowned—experience.

C. The Empire of Experience

This is the criterion of the existentialist. Feelings reign supreme.

The premise is: If it feels good, do it! Or, in the words of Ernest
Hemingway, "What is good is what I feel good after, and what is bad is what I
feel bad after."[11]

The basic assumptions of an existentialist are few but forceful. The present is all-important. As a result, the existentialist seeks to divorce life from the
past and the future. History, traditions and established standards are worthless
and irrelevant. Here is the spring out of which gushes a flood of rebellion.

The existentialist is skeptical of prophecy and any long-range plans for
one's life or for society. The future is unsure. After all, why worry about a
tomorrow threatened by nuclear warfare? The existentialist forgets about
tomorrow. Hear it from one of them. Dr. Alan Watts, writer, philosopher and
interpreter of Zen Buddhism, speaking to a group of students at the Dallas
Memorial Auditorium several years ago on the subject "What if there is no
future?" said, "Get on centre ... live in the eternal now."

More than this, the existentialist is totally sold out to subjectivism. There
is no objective authority beyond oneself. The existentialist lives in a sea of subjectivity. Feelings are all that matter.

Is experience as the ultimate authority an authentic Christian position?

To listen to many Christians one would think so. Recently I heard a brilliant lecture by Dr. Earl Radmacher, president of Western Conservative
Theological Seminary in Portland, Oregon. He spoke of those who use the
testimonial of a changed life as their authority. They say, "It must be right, it
changed my life." Beware my friend! Christianity has no corner on changed
lives. Rennie Davis, one of the Chicago Seven, is a changed man today. How?
He is a devoted disciple of the fifteen-year-old Guru Maharaji ji. Who does

not know of a friend whose life has been revolutionized by Transcendental Meditation or Yoga? Such testimonials conclusively demonstrate that experience, in itself, is no criterion.

Dr. Radmacher further spoke of those who from the pulpit declare their intimate experience with the Lord as final authority. He reminded us of the defender of the faith who marshals several standard proofs of the resurrection of Christ, then concludes, "But the greatest proof of all is this: I spoke with Him today!" Where is the final authority? Experience. You see the pitfall, don't you? What shall we say to the person who says he has never spoken to Him? If his experience is his final authority, he has destroyed the very essence of the Christian faith.

The contemporary version of this experience criteria is expressed most prominently in postmodernism, the present-day reaction to the exalted position modernity (from the eighteenth century Enlightenment) has given to reason and science. In our postmodern world (since the mid-20th century) there is no such thing as absolute truth. Personal experience has replaced the scientific method with its rationalism. Truth is personal, individualistic and relative.

If one's personal experience is the authority, the human race is set adrift on the sea of subjectivity with no compass, chart or anchor. Is this to be accepted as a legitimate Christian position? Not at all.

Though in the philosophical, psychological, sociological and theological fields this "cult of madness" flourishes, it is a usurper of the throne—an illegitimate sovereign.

> Sanctify them in the truth; Thy word is truth. (John 17:17).

> And you shall know the truth, and the truth shall make you free. (John 8:32).

What, then, is the ultimate authority?

D. The Standard of Scripture

This is *Sola Scriptura*. It is the deep and earnest conviction that Scripture is God's holy and infallible Word and that it is the *only* source of revealed theology. It alone is the rule of a Christian's creed and conduct. What it does not determine cannot be said to be a part of Christian truth.

In 1580, in an attempt to effect agreement among the Lutherans, there was prepared the Formula of Concord. It expresses the orthodox Protestant position:

> We believe, teach and confess that the prophetic and apostolic writings of the Old and New Testaments are the only rule and norm according to which all doctrines and teachers alike must be appraised and judged.

This is our answer to the problem of authority.

In the words of the Westminster Confession:

The whole counsel of God, concerning all things necessary for His own glory, man's salvation, faith and life, is either expressly set down in Scripture or by good and necessary consequence, may be deduced from Scripture unto which nothing at any time is added, whether by new revelations of the Spirit, or traditions of men (1:6).

The supreme judge, by which all controversies of religion are to be determined, and all decrees of councils, opinions of ancient writers, doctrines of men, and private spirits, are to be examined and in whose sentence we are to rest, can be no other but by the Holy Spirit speaking in the Scripture (1:10).[12]

In the days of the Reformation, the primary subject under debate was the doctrine of salvation. Yet at the very heart of the Reformation was the matter of authority. The position of the Reformers was simply that the Bible, not the church, not reason and not experience, was the final authority.

On trial for heresy, Martin Luther acknowledged this authority when he said, "I put the Scriptures above all the sayings of the fathers, angels, men and devils. Here I take my stand." Again he said, "My conscience is subject to the Word of God."

The authority of the Scriptures is one of the inescapable implications of revelation and inspiration.

Granted that God did reveal Himself to the human authors (revelation) and that these authors, under the influence of the Holy Spirit, did record accurately what was revealed to them (inspiration), what are the implications for the Scriptures?

We have already asserted the inerrancy of these writings. But there is now another implication. This one will complete our equation.

Revelation + Inspiration = Inerrancy + Authority

If the Bible is a divine revelation that has been God-breathed, then it logically follows that these Scriptures must be absolutely authoritative for every person who names the name of Jesus Christ.

This is more than a logical inference, however.

PROJECT NUMBER 2

The Bible claims to be authoritative. This claim can be supported from four directions.

1. Read: Exodus 31:18; Deuteronomy 4:13; Deuteronomy 10:5; 2 Samuel 23:2. The Old Testament claims such authority for _____.

There are thousands of occurrences of "thus saith the Lord." The religion of Israel was based upon the authority of the written Word of God.

2. Read John 10:35. Much later the Lord claims this same authority for

    _____ .

    B.B. Warfield recognized the depth of this text when he wrote,

    > Now, what is the particular thing in Scripture, for the con-
    > firmation of which the indefectible authority of Scripture is
    > thus invoked? It is one of its most casual clauses—more than
    > that, the very form of its expression is one of its most casual
    > clauses. This means, of course, that in the Saviour's view, the
    > indefectible authority of Scripture attaches to the very form
    > of expression of its most casual clauses. It belongs to
    > Scripture through and through, down to its most minute
    > particulars, that it is of indefectible authority.[13]

    Our Lord recognized its authority when He used it to rebuke Satan (Matt.
    4), when He taught He came to fulfill it (Matt. 5:17), when He submitted to it
    (Matt. 26:24,53,56) and when He taught it to His disciples (Luke 24:27).

3. Read Matthew 24:35.
    It can also be said that the Lord claims authority for _____ .

    Our Lord earlier makes a powerful point when He places His own words
    above the teaching and traditions of Judaism in the Old Testament Scriptures.
    He says, "But I say to you, that every one who looks on a woman to lust for
    her has committed adultery with her already in his heart" (Matt. 5:28).

4. Read 1 Corinthians 14:37; 1 Thessalonians 2:13.
    It is obvious that the apostles claim the full authority of God for

    _____ .

    These apostles were obviously conscious of their delegated authority (Acts
    10:41,42; 1 Thess. 2:13; Gal. 1:1,11,12; 1 Cor. 2:13; 14:37; 2 Cor. 13:3,5,10;
    1 Thess. 5:27; 2 Thess. 3:14). They were foundational in the creation of the
    church (Eph. 2:20) and presented their instructions as from God (2 Cor. 11:4;
    2 John 10). That their authority was so recognized by the early church is clear
    from Acts 2:42 and 2 Peter 3:2.

III. The Ultimate Witness

But what is really the ultimate basis for the Bible's authority? In the final
analysis, the authority of the Bible comes from its author. If it is divine revelation, and if it is God-breathed, then it is absolutely the final authority in every
area of doctrine and practice. The doctrine it teaches comes to us with all the
authority of God Himself. The demands it makes upon daily life patterns
come with all of the authority of God.

This was the fact I sought to establish with Karen that day. The ultimate authority in the life of a Christian is the Word of God. It had become obvious that all my arguments were to no avail. It was just as obvious that the real issue was the question of authority in her life. Finally, in desperation, as a last resort, I turned her to the Bible. Together we looked up 1 Thessalonians 4:3-6. In a hushed voice she read aloud:

> For this is the will of God, your sanctification; that is, that you abstain from sexual immorality; that each of you know how to possess his own vessel in sanctification and honor, not in lustful passion, like the Gentiles who do not know God; and that no man transgress and defraud his brother in the matter because the Lord is the avenger in all these things, just as we also told you before and solemnly warned you.

As she read and reread the verses I waited for the impact. Oh that she would hear it as an authoritative word from God.

In such situations, many times the person has looked up and said, "I am not convinced." How does one become convinced of the authority of the Word of God? Is it by devastating argumentation? Or is it by a dozen proofs? Surely the answer is "No."

What then is the confirmation of its authority?

One of the old theologians, Voetius (1648-1669), has clearly stated the classical doctrine of authority. He says:

> As there is no objective certainty about the authority of Scripture, save as infused and imbued by God the Author of Scripture, so we have no subjective certainty of it, no formal concept of the authority of Scripture, except from God illuminating and convincing inwardly through the Holy Spirit. As Scripture itself, as if radiating an outward principle by its own light (no outsider intervening as principle or means of proof or conviction), is something *aksiopiston* (worthy of belief) or credible *per se* and *in se*—so the Holy Spirit is the inward, supreme, first, independent principle, actually opening and illuminating the eyes of the mind, effectually convincing us of the credible authority of Scripture from it, along with it, and through it, so that being drawn we run, and being passively convinced within, we acquiesce.[14]

For those of us who speak street English, Voetius is simply saying that belief in the authority of Scripture is derived not from argumentation, but from the inner persuasion of the Holy Spirit. This was precisely the position of the Reformers. They believed that the certainty the Bible deserves with us is attained by the testimony of the Spirit.

It is the Holy Spirit in the believer who witnesses to the truth.

And the one who keeps His commandments abides in Him,

and He in him, And we know by this that He abides in us, by the Spirit which He has given us. (1 John 3:24)

While on the one hand the evangelical Christian still cries loudly *Sola Scriptura,* on the other hand he also speaks frequently of the Holy Spirit, the church, reason and experience. How do these relate to each other?

IV. An Important Integration

The ultimate and final authority in the Christian faith is Scripture. The Word of God by virtue of its divine authority is our objective and full authority. This is *Sola Scriptura.*

This authority is confirmed by the witness of the Holy Spirit to those so enlightened by God. The truthfulness and authority of its interpretations are confirmed by the Spirit of God, who inspired them. On the other hand, the objective Scriptures are the authority and they test the genuineness of that which we may think is the witness of the Spirit. The Holy Spirit will never teach or guide in a way that will contradict the Word of God. The Word apart from the Spirit is cold orthodoxy and intellectualism. The Spirit apart from the Scriptures is subjectivism and mysticism. The Spirit confirms the authority of the Word, and the Word tests the authenticity of the Witness.

However, the Holy Spirit indwells the entire Christian community, the church (Eph. 2:22, 1 Cor. 3:16). The authority of the Scriptures and authenticity of any interpretation then, will be confirmed by their widespread or general recognition in the church at large, the community which is so enlightened. However, we certainly must never put the authority of the church above the authority of the Scriptures. The Word of God must always be the test of any interpretation or declaration by the church. But no careful Bible student will ever want to ignore the interpretations of great men of God in ages past.

And what shall we say about reason and Scripture? The authority and integrity of the written Word is clearly confirmed by the enlightened reason of humankind. History, archaeology and science combine with enlightened reason to bear testimony of Scripture. Sir William Herschel, English astronomer and discoverer of the planet Uranus, comments, "All human discoveries seem to be made only for the purpose of confirming more and more strongly the truths that come from on high, and are contained in the sacred writings." Revelation must be examined to be received.

Yet human reason must always be tested by the Bible. Only that which is consistent with divine revelation is valid and reliable. Man's reason stands under God's Word. Reason cannot be the source of truth. It is incapable of inaugurating revealed truth, but it can and must test it.

So it is with the personal experience of believers. Our experiences confirm the Scriptures as the Word of God. A bumper sticker says, "God is not dead, I spoke with Him today." Alfred H. Ackley, the hymn writer, says:

I serve a risen Savior, He's in the world today;
I know that He is living whatever men may say;
I see His hand of mercy, I hear His voice of cheer,
And just the time I need Him He's always near.
He lives, He lives, Christ Jesus lives today!
He walks with me and talks with me along life's narrow way.
He lives, He lives, salvation to impart!
You ask me how I know He lives—?
He lives within my heart.

And yet experience must always be tested by the Word of God and therefore is subject to its authority (1 John 4:1-5). Many people today make extravagant claims of extraordinary experiences. Some are certainly psychologically induced phenomena. Others surely are satanic or demonic. Still others may be of God. Which are from God? Only those that can be tested and proven by the Scriptures! Our subjective experiences must always be subject to the checks of the objective revelation. For example, Paul's experience on the road to Damascus, when he saw the Christ, is controlled by the objective revelation of the resurrection of Christ (1 Cor.15:1-19). It must always be so. And so the relationships can be charted like this:

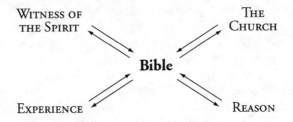

As Karen read and pondered the verses again her eyes became moist. Soon the tears were flowing. The work of the Spirit of God was evident that afternoon. Quietly she was acknowledging the authority of Scripture. Hesitatingly she was bowing to it. What a beautiful sight this is to behold. Unfortunately it is not a common one.

V. The Current Crisis

In an article published in *Interpretation*, Gordon D. Kaufman sadly but correctly wrote:

> The Bible no longer has unique authority for Western man.
> It has become a great archaic monument in our midst… . It
> is no longer the Word of God (if there is a God) to man… .
> Only in rare and isolated pockets—and surely those are rapidly disappearing forever—has the Bible anything like the

kind of existential authority and significance which it once
enjoyed throughout much of Western culture and certainly
among believers.[15]

Why is this so? Why is there such a weak attitude toward the authority of
the Bible today?

Project Number 3

Carefully reflect on the situation in your life, home, church, school and country. What are the major reasons for such a weak attitude toward the authority
of the Scriptures among evangelical Christians today?

1.

2.

3.

4.

The real question that faced my tearful friend that day was a question of
authority. I asked what was the ultimate authority for her life? To be sure, this
question was extremely relevant. Because the area of conduct we were dis-
cussing clearly fell within the scope of Scripture, it could not have been more
appropriate. In many a dilemma, however, the question of authority is entirely
irrelevant.

Have you ever wondered, How far does the authority of the Bible extend?
What is the range of its authority? This is not easily answered, but it cannot
be avoided.

VI. Barbed Boundaries

Obviously its scope is limited. It does not tell me which political party to join.
It does not dictate my career. Many aspects of our social life are apart from its
explicit instructions. Much liberty is granted in the area of recreation, enter-
tainment, styles of dress and means of transportation. It does not declare what
kind of automobile I should drive, what size of house I should purchase or
what type of course I should take in college. Its scope is limited.

However, Scripture does have complete and absolute authority in its own
sphere, that is, "the sphere of the self-revelation of God."

In the words of Geoffrey W. Bromiley:

> Its range is considerable. Historical authority covers the data
> of God's work in history. Theological authority covers the

teachings, not as human ideas about God, but as God's authentic word about Himself. Ethical authority covers the whole range of conduct as it falls under the commandments, injunctions and intentional precedents of the Bible. Liturgical authority covers the practice and worship of the church, preaching the Word, singing God's praise, prayer, administering the sacraments.[16]

Dr. Bromiley goes on to demonstrate that the Word of God also has absolute authority in many secular affairs. We are to "love one another" and "honour the king" and "be subject to every ordinance of man."

The Scriptures, then, are no less comprehensive than they are authoritative. Their scope is broad indeed. They touch my relationship with God, Jesus Christ, the church, my wife, my children, my debtor, my creditor, my employer, an employee, my neighbours, the prime minister, my possessions, the law enforcement officer, the community, the state and so on.

In its own sphere, the Bible is absolutely authoritative. That sphere is broad indeed. It is encircled by biblical barbs that snag the consciences of Christians and dictate direction for our creed and conduct.

One cannot be confronted with such truth as this and walk away from it. It is like a fishhook with barbs so sharp that they dig deep and won't let go. We cannot leave our subject without considering several specific and stinging implications.

VII. Life Responses

After a few moments of quiet reflection Karen raised her eyes to meet mine. Slowly she nodded her head, indicating her response to the Word of God.

Quietly she honoured God in her relationship with her boyfriend. She moved out of his house, found a job and began to grow in the Lord. So did he. A few months later my wife and I heard of their wedding plans. Today they are the centre of a Christian home.

If it is the authoritative Word of God, it calls for life responses. It demands obedience, instant obedience, implicit obedience. There is only one way to live the Christian life. It is "by the Book!"

The acid test of conversion is here. The Master Himself said, "You are My friends, if you do what I command you" (John 15:14).

Hudson Taylor said, "God cannot, will not, does not bless those who are living in disobedience. But only let us set out in the path of obedience, and at once before one stone is laid upon another, God is eager, as it were, to pour out His blessing." Don't settle for anything less.

PROJECT NUMBER 4

1. Discuss the assertion "One can hardly claim to be a Christian who rejects the authority of the Scriptures."

2. What are the implications of this study for the ecumenical movement

today? Can churches who disagree on the principle of authority reach any significant agreement on anything else?

Review

Before you tackle the next chapter take a second look at those questions that prepared the way for this chapter. Don't fool yourself. It will be no waste of time. Read them over once again. Look at them carefully. Can you answer them now? When you have mastered those answers you may want to go a step or two further.

FOR FURTHER STUDY

1. What are the objective tests for determining whether or not a person is speaking the truth by the Spirit of God or error by a demonic or human spirit? (1 John 4:1-5)

2. Evaluate the beliefs of the Jehovah's Witnesses by the orthodox Protestant criterion of *Sola Scriptura*.

END NOTES

[1] James I. Packer, *Fundamentalism and the Word of God* (Grand Rapids, MI: Wm. B. Eerdmans Publishing Co., 1970), p.42.

[2] *Ibid.*, p.44.

[3] *Ibid.*, pp.44-46.

[4] *Ibid.*, p.50.

[5] *Ibid.*, p.49.

[6] *Ibid.*, p.49.

[7] Loraine Boettner, *Roman Catholicism* (Philadelphia, PA: The Presbyterian and Reformed Publishing Co., 1962), p.77.

[8] Clark H. Pinnock, *Biblical Revelation* (Chicago, IL: Moody Press, 1971), p.124.

[9] Loraine Boettner, *Roman Catholicism*, pp.78,79

[10] *Ibid.*, p.79.

[11] Joseph Fletcher, *Situation Ethics* (Philadelphia, PA: The Westminster Press), p.54.

[12] Clark H. Pinnock, *Biblical Revelation*, p.114.

[13] Benjamin B. Warfield, *The Inspiration and Authority of the Bible* (Philadelphia, PA: The Presbyterian and Reformed Publishing Company, 1970), p.140.

[14] Bernard Ramm, *The Witness of the Spirit* (Grand Rapids, MI: Wm. B. Eerdmans Publishing Company, 1959), pp.69,70.

[15] Gordon D. Kaufman, "What Shall We Do With The Bible?" *Interpretation* (January, 1971), pp.95-112.

[16] Geoffrey W. Bromiley, "The Inspiration and Authority of Scripture," *Eternity* (August, 1970), p.20.

BIBLIOGRAPHY

Boettner, Loraine. *Roman Catholicism*. Philadelphia, PA: The Presbyterian and Reformed Publishing Co., 1962.

Fletcher, Joseph. *Situation Ethics*. Philadelphia, PA: The Westminster Press, 1966.

Henry, Carl F.H. (ed.). *Revelation and the Bible*. Grand Rapids, MI: Wm. B. Eerdmans Publishing Co., 1970.

Packer, James I. *Fundamentalism and the Word of God*. Grand Rapids, MI: Wm. B. Eerdmans Publishing Co., 1970.

Phillips, J.B. *Ring of Truth*. New York, NY: The MacMillan Co., 1967.

Pinnock, Clark H. *Biblical Revelation*. Chicago, IL: Moody Press, 1971.

Warfield, B.B. *The Inspiration and Authority of the Bible*. Philadelphia, PA: The Presbyterian and Reformed Publishing Co., 1970.

Part V

CANONIZATION

CHAPTER SIX

ৠ

THE COLLECTION BEGINS

Preparing the Way

1. Distinguish between "canon" and "canonicity."

2. What is the sole criterion for canonicity?

3. Is there a test of inspiration? What is it?

4. What part does the providence of God play in canonicity?

5. What were the three major divisions of the Hebrew Old Testament? How many books were in each division?

6. Who was responsible for this structure of the Hebrew Old Testament canon? When was it finally formed?

7. What is the significance of our Lord's testimony to the Law, the Prophets and the Psalms in Luke 24:44?

8. What were the four classes of literature that were present in the Old Testament era?

9. Define "Apocrypha." Describe the content and value of the Apocrypha.

10. Why do evangelical Protestants not regard the Apocrypha as canonical?

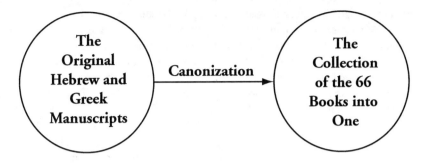

Some time ago "Ron," a local high school teacher, staggered into my office in a mild state of shock. He looked as though he had just tackled a tiger and lost. That was about it too. He needed help fast. Just that day he had been sharing his faith with a colleague and had been shot down in flames. In the heat of the battle Ron's associate had challenged his authority—the Bible. Although it was an old argument, my friend had never met it before. It obviously had knocked him off balance. His fellow teacher had simply rejected the Bible. This wasn't what sent my friend reeling however. It was the reason.

According to his antagonist, the Bible is merely a collection of books put together by men long after the days of Christ. He noted there was little agreement among these men. Different collections exist. "How do you know your Bible contains all the books it should contain?" he asked. He pointed out that there may be other worthy books overlooked! He wondered how Ron could be sure that some unworthy books had not been unwarrantedly placed in the collection. Some may have been included by mistake!

My beleaguered and beaten friend needed some answers. Who did the collecting? Can we be sure the collection is a reliable one? Why do we have sixty-six books in our Bible instead of sixty-four? Are there some that really don't belong there? Why do we have sixty-six instead of the seventy-seven found in some Bibles? Are there some that have been lost or that we have failed to recognize?

These questions relate to the canon of Scripture—the subject of our study in this and the following chapter.

To hold his own in the teachers' lounge that day, Ron needed answers to these very questions. He needed some background. He had to understand the process in order to eliminate the problems. A few simple facts would quickly dislodge his colleague from his rather pompous pedestal.

I. A Word of Explanation

The term "canon" is derived from a Greek word meaning a staff, straight rod, rule or standard. This Greek word was derived in turn from the Sumerian word that originally meant a "reed" (Job 40:21). Because reeds were often used as measuring sticks, in a figurative sense the word implied straightness or uprightness and was used for a measuring standard or norm. It was not until c. A.D. 352 that the word was first used by Athanasius in reference to the divinely inspired books of Scripture. The "canon" therefore is the collection of writings that constitute the authoritative and final norm, rule, or standard for our faith and practice. In short, the canon comprises the writings of the Bible, both the Old and New Testaments. The Bible is called the canon because it is the objective rule for measuring, or judging, all matters of doctrine and life.

If the word "canon" implies the status of the Bible by virtue of its inspiration, the word "canonicity" often applies to the recognition of this status by the church. It is the process by which the various books of the Bible were brought together and their value as the Word of God recognized. One scholar speaks of canonicity as "the churches' recognition of the authority and extent of inspired writings."[1]

Perhaps the most helpful way to get a hold on this immense topic is to slice it in half. Surely the most appropriate place to apply the knife is at the very point of division in our English Bible. In this lesson, then, we will concentrate only upon the collection of the Hebrew manuscripts in our Old Testament.

II. The Test

It is obvious that the thirty-nine books of our Old Testament constitute only a small part of the literature that came from the pens of the children of Israel before Christ. There are such books as 1 and 2 Maccabees, the Wisdom of Solomon, Ecclesiasticus, books we today call the Apocrypha. There are such books as the Assumption of Moses and the Book of Enoch and several others that we call the Pseudepigrapha. There are a number of pieces of interesting literature from the Qumran community of the Essenes, such as the Manual of Discipline. Why are some of these not recognized as canonical? What is the test of canonicity?

The simple test for canonicity is inspiration. The writings that are inspired by God the Holy Spirit constitute the norm, or standard, of faith and practice. In ancient days it was its inspiration that made a book authoritative and because of this authority it was recognized as canonical. That is to say, a book did not become part of the canon because it was recognized as such. Rather, it was recognized as such because it was part of the canon by virtue of inspiration. The moment an inspired book was written it was canonical. The authors were certainly conscious of this, as is testified by their frequent use of "thus saith the Lord." These writings were immediately held as authoritative by some, and probably deposited in the temple. But how were others to recognize which books were inspired and canonical and which were not? This was no simple question.

To say that the sole test for their recognition and acceptance was inspiration is to answer our question correctly but not completely. This simply raises another question, What is the test of inspiration?

Gleason Archer states it succinctly when he says,

> The only true test of canonicity which remains is the testimony of God the Holy Spirit to the authority of His own Word. This testimony found a response of recognition, faith and submission in the hearts of God's people who walked in covenant fellowship with Him.[2]

E.J. Young agrees when he says,

> The canonical books of the Old Testament were divinely revealed and their authors were holy men who spoke as they were borne of the Holy Ghost. In His good providence God brought it about that His people should recognize and receive His Word. How He planted this conviction in their hearts with respect to the identity of His Word we may not be able fully to understand or explain.[3]

We conclude, therefore, that the books that were inspired by the Holy Spirit, and therefore were canonical, were recognized by men of faith as the Holy Spirit bore witness to the authority of these writings in their hearts.

Three crucial elements are involved in this test.

1. The work of the Holy Spirit in inspiration.

2. The witness of the Holy Spirit to what He has inspired and is therefore authoritative.

3. The providence of God, which becomes apparent in the recognition, collection and preservation of the canonical books.

These factors constitute three basic steps.

PROJECT NUMBER 1

1. On the chart below, label the appropriate steps with the above three points.

2. Match the following terms to the appropriate steps: Collection, Inspiration and Canonicity.

III. The Finished Product

To understand this process is to be equipped to cope with dozens of questions similar to those that struck down Ron. With the process firmly fixed in our minds we are ready to look at the product in the Old Testament.

The Hebrew text of the Old Testament contains three major divisions. Take a careful look at them. How do they differ from the Old Testament you know?

Law (five books):
  • Genesis, Exodus, Leviticus, Numbers, Deuteronomy.

Prophets (eight books):
  • Former: Joshua, Judges, Samuel, Kings.
  • Latter: Isaiah, Jeremiah, Ezekiel, The Twelve (Minor Prophets).

Writings (eleven books):
  • Poetry and Wisdom: Psalms, Proverbs, Job
  • Rolls: Song of Solomon, Ruth, Lamentations, Ecclesiastes, Esther.
  • History: Daniel, Ezra/Nehemiah, Chronicles.

What are your observations? By way of comparison, you see every one of your thirty-nine Old Testament books represented here. That is very important to note. In contrast to your Bible, however, you see only three major divisions, not four. The order of books is quite different from your Bible today. You have even seen a difference in the number of books. The combination of writings resulted in only twenty-four books. This was not the only combination that existed in ancient times. When Josephus speaks of twenty-two Old Testament sacred books, he is simply reflecting another structure or order of the same twenty-four (or, if you like, thirty-nine) books.[4]

In the Greek translation of the Hebrew Old Testament, the Septuagint, the books are arranged more or less topically. They fall into four divisions: the books of the law, history, poetry and wisdom, and prophecy. In general the Latin Vulgate follows the Septuagint. It is this order that has been adopted in our Protestant English Bible.

An understanding of the finished product, the Hebrew canon with its three divisions, was of critical importance to Ron. It offers tremendous leverage in defending the Bible against the kind of attack he faced. To use it effectively, however, Ron needed to know not only the facts of a threefold division in the Hebrew canon, but also the details of its formation.

IV. The Great Assembly

Although it is impossible to positively date the origin of this threefold division of the Old Testament canon, Jewish tradition dates it from the time of Ezra, attributing the work to him and the men of the Great Assembly, 520 B.C. This assembly gave way to the Sanhedrin around 300 B.C. This dates the divisions then, from about the fifth century B.C. If this is so, apparently the division was not rigidly held. The Old Testament canon is described in the New Testament as "the law and the prophets" (Luke 24:27). However, our Lord does refer to this threefold division in Luke 24:44.

The basis for this threefold division has been the object of much discussion. The first division was determined by the sole authorship of Moses. These five books constitute the "law of Moses." He is recognized as the greatest of the prophets of Israel, the lawgiver of the nation. They were undoubtedly gathered by Joshua and regarded by the nation as the word of God from that date forward.

The second division is called the "prophets," a title that is appropriate according to every indication of their authorship. These books were written by men with the gift of prophecy who occupied the office of prophet in the nation. As these prophets were under Moses in the administration of the nation it is appropriate that their books form the second division.

The third division comprises books of a variety of material written by men who did not occupy the official office of prophet. This explains why Daniel's book is in the last division rather than the second one. Its position among the "writings" does not suggest a late date as many critics say. Status in that second division was based upon the official status of the authors in the nation.[5]

As the inspired books in the second and third divisions were written they were, by virtue of their inspiration, canonical. That is, they were authoritative. They were a standard for the faith and practice of Israel. In the providence of God and by the witness of the Spirit, these books were recognized by men of faith as authoritative. They were securely preserved in the temple precincts until the time of the Great Assembly when, under God, the twenty-four books were collected together and set in the order of the Hebrew Old Testament.

V. What Is the Point?

If you are wondering what the point of giving you all this historical data and detail, let me clear up the matter right now. We have just established that by the sixth century B.C., the Jewish community had recognized and collected twenty-four books (thirty-nine, by our count) that they regarded as authoritative. These were organized in three major divisions. They were the standard for their creed and conduct. Here was their canon.

This simple summary has the support of a host of witnesses. Consider but a few.

The earliest extant reference to these three divisions comes from the prologue of the apocryphal Ecclesiasticus. There we read, "Whereas many and great things have been delivered to us by the Law and the Prophets, and by others that have followed their steps ..." Here the authors of the third division are described as those who have followed in the steps of the prophets.

The testimony of Josephus, the first-century Jewish historian, speaks of the very thirty-nine books of our Old Testament as the corpus of Scripture "which are justly believed to be divine." When he speaks of twenty-two books, he simply reflects a different structure of ordering the books.[6]

Philo, a learned Jew of Alexandria, refers to or uses as authoritative all the books of the Old Testament except five (Esther, Ezekiel, Daniel, Ecclesiastes, Song of Solomon). These are never denied, just ignored. On the other hand he never quotes nor mentions any of the apocryphal books.

Among the Dead Sea Scrolls discovered in 1947, some portion of all the thirty-nine books of our Old Testament were found. They obviously held these books in high esteem and regarded them as authoritative. Although other literature is alluded to, it is never quoted as authoritative. The books written by the Qumran sect make no claim of inspiration for themselves.[7]

Following the destruction of Jerusalem, Jamnia became a centre for scriptural study under Rabbi Johanan ben Zakkal. Here discussion continued concerning the canonicity of certain books that were disputed. Although the so-called Council of Jamnia (A.D. 90) was something less than a formal council, informal discussions were held that helped to crystallize and fix more firmly the Jewish tradition. It has been demonstrated that this "council" was actually "confirming public opinion not forming it."[8] Here the extent of the Old Testament canon seems to have been finally and forever settled. The same twenty-four books set in three divisions five hundred years earlier were confirmed as canonical!

Before you press on, place yourself in Ron's position for a few moments. With the background of this chapter can you answer these questions?

PROJECT NUMBER 2

1. In the Old Testament era did different collections exist?

2. Was the collection of Old Testament books made long after the writings of those books?

3. How do you know that your Old Testament contains all the inspired books of that time, and only inspired books?

If Ron's colleague was both skilful and knowledgeable, he would still have one trump card left in his hand. It is used with devastating success over and over again against Christians who are unskilled and without knowledge.

VI. What about the Apocrypha?

Several of our new versions of the Bible include the Apocrypha. What is it? Why is it included only in some versions? Is it part of the Word of God? Answers to these questions and more come more easily when we understand that the Apocrypha is only one of the four classes of literature that emerged in the Old Testament era.

A. The Homolegoumena

These were "the acknowledged books." Thirty-four of our Old Testament books were accepted as canonical by men of faith when they were written, and their canonicity was never disputed. They were universally and commonly acknowledged as authoritative writings inspired of God.

B. Antilegoumena

Five of our Old Testament books were "books spoken against." They were apparently accepted immediately by believers as canonical, but at a later date were questioned as to their place in the canon. Surprisingly we have no record of any of these books being questioned until the first century A.D.

Ecclesiastes was disputed because of its alleged pessimism, Epicurianism and denial of life to come. In the light of its purpose and literary technique, these objections are not valid.

Esther was disputed because the name of God does not appear in it. This objection is offset by the spectacular manifestation of divine providence and a recognition of the peculiar purpose of the book. It is to present the fortunes of Israel in unbelief. Because they are in unbelief God withdraws from direct communication and works providentially.

The *Song of Solomon* was criticized because of its low morality. It speaks of physical attractiveness in rather startling and bold terms. The interpretation of Hillel, who identified Solomon with Jehovah and the Shulamite with Israel, added a spiritual dimension that helped overcome the objections.

Ezekiel was challenged on the basis of the contradiction between the description of his temple in the latter chapters of the book and the temple of Jerusalem, which had been built by Zerubbabel. This objection was met by the observation that the differences were minor and the suggestion that Ezekiel may be speaking of a future temple, as indeed he is—the millennial temple.

The objections to *Proverbs* were based upon several minor, apparent contradictions. For example, "Answer not a fool according to his folly" (26:4) and "Answer a fool according to his folly" (26:5).

C. Pseudepigrapha

These are religious books written under the assumed name of a biblical character such as Moses, Enoch and others. These books were written in times of national emergencies, as in the persecution of the Jews by Antiochus. Their purpose was to encourage the morale of the people. The four types of literature found in this category were apocalyptic, legendary, political and didactic. They were never recognized as canonical.

In Jude 14-16, the pseudepigrapha book of Enoch is quoted. This book of Enoch never claimed canonicity. It is, however, quoted as a true statement.

The apostle recognizes truth in this writing as we today would recognize it in a poem by Robert Frost or in the writing of C.S. Lewis. As this truth may be quoted in a sermon, so Jude found truth in the Book of Enoch and quoted it.

D. Apocrypha

Fourteen books written between 200 B.C. and A.D. 100, mainly by Alexandrian Jews, are known by the term Apocrypha, which in classical Greek means "obscure" or "incomprehensible" or "hidden." Jerome used the word for spurious, non-canonical books.

The books fall into five classifications:

> The Wisdom Books—Wisdom of Solomon, Ecclesiasticus
> The Historical Books—1 Esdras, 1 & 2 Maccabees
> The Religious Romances—Tobit, Judith
> The Prophetic Books—Baruch, 2 Esdras
> The Legendary Additions
> - Prayer of Manasseh
> - Remainder of Esther
>   - Songs of Three Holy Children
> - History of Susanna
> - Bel and the Dragon

All of these are accepted by the Roman Catholic Church today, except 1 and 2 Esdras and the Prayer of Manasseh.

Although these books were not recognized by the Aramaic Targums* and the earliest Syriac Peshitta,† yet they are included in the Septuagint—the Greek translation of the Old Testament by the Alexandrian Jews. Does the presence of the Apocrypha in the Septuagint indicate they were recognized as canonical?

Not necessarily. Several points ought to be noted.

1. The manuscript evidence is uncertain. Vaticanus lacks 1, 2 Maccabees, includes 1 Esdras. Sinaiticus lacks Baruch, includes 4 Maccabees. Alexandrius contains 1 Esdras, 3 and 4 Maccabees. "Thus it turns out that even the three earliest manuscripts of the LXX show considerable uncertainty as to which books constitute the list of Apocrypha, and that the fourteen accepted by the Roman church are by no means substantiated by the testimony of the great uncials of the fourth and fifth centuries."[9] The first point to be noticed, then, is that there never was a definite canon of the Septuagint.

2. Philo, the Alexandrian historian, never quotes from the Apocrypha. This is surprising because he lived in the city of the Septuagint, which included it.

---

* Aramaic Targums—Aramaic paraphrases or interpretations of some parts of the Old Testament.

† Syriac Peshitta—The Syrian translation of the Old Testament Scriptures. Peshitta = "simple." A simple translation.

3. The discoveries at Qumran, where some apocryphal books and pseudepi-
    graphic‡ books have been found, along with books accepted as canonical,
    demonstrate that "subcanonical books may be preserved and utilized
    along with canonical books."[10] Therefore the presence of the Apocrypha
    in the Septuagint does not necessarily imply that believers recognized it as
    canonical.

4. The Septuagint was the Bible of our Lord and the early church. Yet never
    did our Lord or the writers of the New Testament quote from the apoc-
    ryphal books that were interwoven through the Bible they used. Never
    did they indicate any recognition of authority in these books.

5. Aquila's Greek Version of the Old Testament (A.D. 128) did not contain
    the Apocrypha and yet was accepted by the Jews of Alexandria.

6. In his Latin Vulgate, Jerome included the Apocrypha but did not recog-
    nize it as canonical. He pleaded for the recognition of only the Hebrew
    canon, excluding the Apocrypha.

7. Meliot, Justin Martyr, Origen, Tertullian, Gregory the Great (640),
    Cardinal Ximenes and Cardinal Cajetan (1534) all rejected the canonicity
    of the Apocrypha.

However, in 1546, at the Council of Trent, the Roman Catholic church
decreed the Apocrypha to be "Sacrosancta." "At one of the prolonged sessions,
with only fifty-three prelates present, not one of whom was a scholar distinguished for historical learning, the decree 'Sacrosancta' was passed, which
declared the Old Testament including the Apocrypha are of God."[11] In so
doing Rome disregarded not only the testimony of history, which generally
rejected the Apocrypha, but also the role of the church councils, which up to
this point had only confirmed the opinion of people. These councils never
formed public opinion, they only confirmed it. Why were such precedents
neglected? Some historians think Rome was motivated by political reasons. In
the wake of the Reformation she needed to reassert the authority of the
church.

Merrill F. Unger offers a helpful survey of the history of the Apocrypha
since 1546.

> The Church of England (1562) followed Jerome's words, "The
> Church doth read … (the Apocrypha) for example of life and
> instruction of manners; but yet doth it not apply them to estab-
> lish any doctrine." The view of the Westminster Confession
> would logically banish them from the Bible altogether. "The
> books commonly called Apocrypha, not being of divine inspi-

---

‡ Pseudepigraphic books—These were other Jewish writings that were excluded from the Old Testament canon
and from the Apocrypha.

ration, are not part of the canon of Scripture; and therefore are of no authority in the Church of God, nor to be otherwise approved and made use of than other human writings." This view may be said to have prevailed in Protestantism.

Beginning in 1629, the Apocrypha were omitted from some editions of English Bibles. Since 1827, they have been excluded from practically all editions. In the Revised Version (1885) and the American Standard Revision (1901), they were omitted entirely. In 1895, they were revised and published in a separate volume.[12]

In the ecumenical climate of our day, the Apocrypha is becoming increasingly popular and is included in many translations of the Bible. For example, the New English Bible and the Oxford Annotated Bible include it. Should the Apocrypha be regarded as inspired and occupy a place in the canon of Scripture? For several reasons we think not.

1. Not one of the apocryphal books was at any time included in the Hebrew canon.

2. Not one is ever quoted in the New Testament. This is truly amazing because they were included in the Septuagint—the Bible of the apostles! The Greek Bible (in its extent) was not the Bible of the Lord and disciples. Although they used it, they did not use it all! It is not entirely clear whether the prophecy attributed to Enoch in Jude 14 is a reference to the Enoch of Genesis 5 or to a similar statement in the Book of Enoch (1:9). If it is from the Book of Enoch, it is important to note that it is not from an apocrypha book, but rather from the pseudopigrapha books (see p. 99). Furthermore, the book never claimed canoncity and was never recognized as canonical. As Paul quoted a Cretan poet in Titus 1:12 so Jude quotes something as true from the book of Enoch.

3. These books do not claim to be the word of God. As a matter of fact Maccabees denies he is a prophet. Upon at least three occasions (1 Macc. 4:46; 9:27; 14:41) he indicates that the current feeling in Israel was that there was no prophet available for consultation. He recognized that the spirit of prophecy had long since departed.

4. The testimony of Josephus indicates that the Jews believed the Old Testament canon to be closed and the gift of prophecy to have ceased in the fifth century B.C. In his *Contra Opionem* Josephus writes:

    From Artaxerxes (the successor of Xerxes) until our time everything has been recorded, but has not been deemed worthy of like credit with what preceded, because the exact succession of the prophets ceased. But what faith we have placed in our own writings is evident by our conduct; for though so long a time has now passed, no one has dared to add anything to them, or to take anything from them, or to alter anything in them.[13]

Here Josephus reflects the minds of the first century Jews and says no canonical writings have been composed from the time of Artaxerxes, which, by the way, was the time of Malachi.

5. The quality and doctrine of the Apocrypha is very inferior to that of the canonical books. It has well been pointed out that

both Judith and Tobit contain historical, chronological and geographical errors. The books justify falsehood and deception and make salvation to depend upon works of merit. Almsgiving, for example, is said to deliver from death (Tob. 12:9; 4:10; 14:10,11).

Judith lives a life of falsehood and deception in which she is represented as assisted by God (9:10,13). Ecclesiasticus and the Wisdom of Solomon inculcate a morality based upon expediency. Wisdom teaches the creation of the world out of pre-existent matter (11:17). Ecclesiasticus teaches that the giving of alms makes atonement for sin (3:30).

In Barach it is said that God hears the prayers for the dead (3:4), and in I Maccabees there are historical and geographical errors.[14]

This is not to say the Apocrypha is of no value. Although they are not Scripture, the books are of "considerable antiquity and of real value. They, like the Dead Sea Scrolls, are monuments to Jewish literary activity of the intertestamental period."[15] They show the lack of idolatry, the solid monotheism and the presence of a Messianic hope in the period between the Testaments. Also, they trace the heroic political struggles of Israel for liberty.

The material of this chapter is part of the very material I put into the hands of my anxious friend Ron. But it is only part. There still remains those gnawing questions about the New Testament that call for an answer. It is amazing how an experience like his in that teachers' lounge sharpens one's appetite for this kind of information! Armed with some facts, Ron was able to "return to the scene" and "contend for the faith." And this is the calling of every believer.

Review

In this chapter we have established a definition for the term "canon" and have studied the test, the divisions and the extent of the Old Testament canon. Have you grasped the key points? Why not test yourself now? Go back to the questions at the beginning of our chapter and measure your retention. You ought to be able to answer every one of them now.

FOR FURTHER STUDY

1. Study carefully Jude 14-16. What is the problem here? How can it be answered?

2. Discuss the liberal theories as to the origin of the Old Testament canon. See: Gleason Archer, *A Survey of Old Testament Introduction*, (Chicago, IL: Moody Press, 1964), pp.70-72.

3. Explain and refute the documentary theory of the Pentateuch. See again Gleason Archer, *A Survey of Old Testament Introduction*, chs.6-8.

END NOTES

[1] Dr. S.L. Johnson, Jr., "New Testament Introduction" (Unpublished class notes, Dallas Theological Seminary, 1966).

[2] Gleason Archer, *A Survey of Old Testament Introduction* (Chicago, IL: Moody Press, 1964), p.69.

[3] E.J. Young, "The Canon of the Old Testament," *Revelation and the Bible,* ed. Carl F.H. Henry (Grand Rapids, MI: Baker Book House, 1958), p.168.

[4] Laird Harris, *Inspiration and Canonicity of the Bible* (Grand Rapids, MI: Zondervan Publishing House, 1969), p.141.

[5] Gleason Archer, *A Survey of Old Testament Introduction,* pp.368,369.

[6] Laird Harris, *Inspiration and Canonicity of the Bible,* p.141.

[7] *Ibid.,* p.137.

[8] R.K. Harrison, *Introduction to the Old Testament* (Grand Rapids, MI: Wm. B. Eerdmans Publishing Company, 1969), p.278.

[9] Gleason Archer, *A Survey of Old Testament Introduction,* p.66.

[10] *Ibid.,* p.66.

[11] Merrill F. Unger, *Introductory Guide to the Old Testament* (Grand Rapids, MI: Zondervan Publishing House, 1964), p.106.

[12] *Ibid.,* p.107

[13] Gleason Archer, *A Survey of Old Testament Introduction,* p.63.

[14] E.J. Young, "The Canon of The Old Testament," pp.167,168.

[15] Laird Harris, *Inspiration and Canonicity of the Bible,* p.180.

BIBLIOGRAPHY

Archer, Gleason. *A Survey of Old Testament Introduction.* Chicago, IL: Moody Press, 1964.

Beckwith, Robert. *The Old Testament Canon of the New Testament Church.* Grand Rapids, MI: Wm. B. Eerdmans Publishing Co., 1985.

Harris, Laird. *Inspiration and Canonicity of the Bible.* Grand Rapids, MI: Zondervan Publishing House, 1969.

Harrison, R.K. *Introduction to the Old Testament.* Grand Rapids, MI: Wm. B. Eerdmans Publishing Company, 1969.

Henry, Carl F.H. (ed.). *Revelation and the Bible.* Grand Rapids, MI: Baker Book House, 1958.

Unger, Merrill F. *Introductory Guide to the Old Testament.* Grand Rapids, MI: Zondervan Publishing House, 1964.

Van Campenhausen, Hans. *The Formation of the Christian Bible.* Philadelphia, PA: Fortress Press, 1972.

Waltke, Bruce. "How We Got Our Old Testament," *Christian History,* Vol. XIII, No.3, Issue 43, pp.32,33.

CHAPTER SEVEN

ॐ

A TANTALIZING QUESTION

Preparing the Way

1. What factors gave rise to the need for a New Testament? After all, the Old Testament was sufficient for Israel for hundreds of years.

2. What is the single criterion to be considered in recognizing any book as part of the canon of Scripture?

3. In determining whether or not a book is inspired, five questions must be asked. What are they?

4. Mark out the three stages in the formation of the New Testament canon. What were the important characteristics of each phase?

5. Who was the first person to publish a complete list of the New Testament books as we know them today? What is the date?

6. What was the express purpose of the early church councils? What role did they play in the process of canonization?

7. What four classes of literature were present in the early centuries of the church age?

8. What changes took place in the extent of the canon as a result of the Council of Trent?

9. Why is the Book of Mormon not accepted as part of the canon of Scripture?

10. What three lines of testimony can be drawn to support the idea of a closed and complete canon of Scripture?

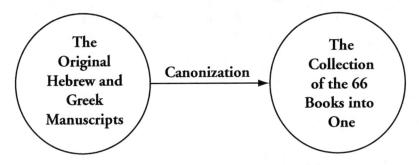

It was at the request of a young lady in our chapel that the appointment was set up. We agreed on a time later that week in my office. Its purpose was clearly defined. I was to explain my Christian faith to two young Mormon missionaries! When my young friend had witnessed to them the previous week, they seemed open and responsive. She was anxious to pursue the contact and I became involved.

At the precise prearranged time they arrived. One was slightly older than the other, but neither of them could have seen his twentieth birthday yet. Impeccably groomed, they entered my office. Their courteous and gracious manners commended them highly. My skepticism about the appointment began to recede. I thought this could be a real breakthrough for God!

My hopes, however, were soon to be dashed to pieces. After a brief word of prayer, I began to present the case for the good news of our Lord Jesus. And what do you think? Not a word of protest was raised by either of my young guests. Worse than that, there was total agreement. I say worse than that, because I have long since learned that little progress is made in evangelism if there is no sense of need.

And my two guests displayed no sense of need whatsoever. They just agreed with everything I said.

Then came the second round. After I had presented my case with no evident effect, they took the initiative. Their case was simple. They believed everything that was in our Bible (which bluff, by the way, I was later able to penetrate and destroy), but went one step further. They also believed what God had given through Joseph Smith. Finally we came to grips with the issue. They claimed that their Book of Mormon is a revelation from God with inspiration and authority equal to the Bible. As a matter of fact they claimed that it not only complemented the teachings of the Bible, but also supplemented them. At this point they became very aggressive, pressing their point home with great fervour. I was told, "If you are a Bible-believing North American Christian, there is a further word from God for you in the Book of Mormon."

Is this possible? How will we answer such a proposition? Was the canon of Scripture closed at the end of the first century? Could God give us a further revelation? Has He? Is our Bible a complete or incomplete revelation? Is the canon closed or open?

Answers to these questions demand some understanding of the entire process of canonicity—especially as it relates to the New Testament. It is to this task that we now turn.

It has well been said that "The Christian church was born with a canon in her hands."[1] Because the apostles and early Christians were rooted in Judaism, the idea of a canon was not foreign to them. They had never been without an objective authoritative corpus of Scripture. They had the Old Testament. Soon it became apparent that this was neither sufficient nor complete.

I. Four Factors

But why? What was the need for a New Testament? Four major factors contributed to its emergence.

First, there were the authoritative words of Christ. Although our Lord acknowledged the authority of the Old Testament canon (Matt. 4:4,7; 5:18; John 10:35; Luke 24:44), yet He placed His own words beside the Old Testament Scriptures as equally authoritative. On six occasions in Matthew 5 He placed His word on a par with the Old Testament saying, "Ye have heard that it was said … But I say unto you …" (Matt. 5:21,27,31,33,38,43). He was fully aware of His authority and this awareness dawned upon others also. The people who heard Him "were amazed at His teaching, for He was teaching them as *one* having authority, and not as the scribes" (Mark 1:22). Luke, among others, recognized His authority when he wrote of "all that Jesus began to do and teach" (Acts 1:1). If the authority of Christ was to be placed beside the Old Testament as He claimed and as others believed, then the need for another collection of writings, which contained His words, bore His authority and testified to His Person and work, was obvious.

Second, the birth of the church demanded a charter for this new creation. It must have soon been apparent to the early church that God was starting something new and doing something different at Pentecost. He had spoken of building His Church (Matt. 16:18), destroying the temple (Matt. 24:2) and dispersing the nation (Luke 21:24). Acts 2 records the birthday of the church. It was the beginning of an entirely new entity (Eph. 3:2b). In this church there was a freedom from the old laws of Judaism. The need for a canon to govern the practice of this new entity quickly arose. As the nation of Israel needed an authoritative constitution when it was formed, so the need for a canon of Scripture for this new work of God—the church—was immediately recognized.

Third, certain problems within the church itself called for a New Testament. Controversy over doctrinal issues was not uncommon (Gal. 1:8). An authoritative norm for the doctrine of the church was imperative. Within half a century there was an abundance of religious writings within the grasp of Christians. Again, a collection was necessary to distinguish the authoritative from the unauthoritative. Practical questions regarding public worship in the churches were being asked (e.g., 1 Thess. 5:27). The inevitable and pressing question became, Which books ought to be read and taught in the churches?

Finally, political events in the first centuries not only intensified the need for recognizing those books that were inspired and authoritative, but even forced this process. When Diocletian ordered all the books destroyed in A.D. 303 the questions arose, Which ones should be saved? Which books are we willing to die for?

In a thousand areas "necessity is the mother of invention." In this case, a fourfold necessity provided the spiritual environment for the rise of the New Testament.

Project Number 1

Enter a time tunnel that will situate you, for a few moments, in the midst of a first-century church. You know only of the Old Testament and the preaching of the apostles. What specific questions would you have been asking? What particular need for a New Testament would you have felt?

Again it must be said that the one test for canonicity is inspiration. It was not the decree of a council that gave a book authority. Rather it was its authority that spurred the collection. This authority is inherent in inspiration. An inspired book is authoritative and therefore canonical when written.

But isn't this begging the question? This line of reasoning cries out for a test for inspiration. How did they know which books were inspired and therefore authoritative and canonical?

II. Five Critical Questions

The primary factor was the internal witness of the Holy Spirit to Spirit-led believers who read and studied the books. The Spirit of God, Who had taken up residence within the believers, testified positively to what He had inspired as they read it.

> He is the Spirit of truth—John 14:17.

> He guides us into all truth—John 16:13.

So the first question that was asked was this: Is there the witness of the Spirit in the Christian community that this is an inspired book?

There was a second question: Is the book apostolic in origin? Was it written by an apostle, such as the Gospels of Matthew and John? Was it written by someone who had direct contact with an apostle, like Mark who knew Peter closely, or Luke who knew Paul well?

Apostles were students under our Lord's teaching for three years. They were eyewitnesses of His resurrection. They had spent with Him those wonderful forty days of instruction before the ascension. They were commissioned by Him and spoke with the authority of Jesus Himself. The very term "apostle" means one commissioned to speak and act with the authority of the One who sent Him. The early church fathers recognized the authority of apostles. Ignatius of Antioch wrote in A.D. 117, "I do not, as Peter and Paul, issue commandments to you. They were apostles, I am but a condemned man."[2] In A.D. 95, Clement of Rome wrote, "The apostles received the Gospel for us from the Lord Jesus Christ. Jesus was sent forth from God, so then Christ is from God and the apostles from Christ."[3]

The third question was, Do the contents of the book agree with the teachings of Jesus, and do they present a high view of the person and work of Christ?

Believers were not to believe every spirit, but were to test the spirits. The test of the Holy Spirit is that He testifies that Jesus Christ is come in the flesh. That is, He testifies clearly to both the deity and humanity of Jesus Christ. Any book that denies these truths is not inspired by the Spirit of God.

The fourth question was, Is it authentic? Is it what it claims to be? Was it written by whom it claims to be written? Did it originate in the place it claims to have originated? Did Paul really write it? Was it actually written from Rome? Was it really written to Timothy?

The final question was this: Is there a widespread acceptance of its authority by the Christian Church?

If it was a genuinely inspired book, there would surely be a widespread recognition of that fact through the witness of the Spirit. The recognition of a book, then, did not rest in the hands of a few men or some radical group. It depended upon a widespread acceptance of the book. This acceptance was expressed at church councils where representatives from every country listed the books recognized in their area.

By the very nature of the case, this question injected an extensive time factor into the process of recognition. The book of 3 John, written to an individual, would take longer to be widely circulated and accepted than the epistle to the Ephesians, which was written as a circular letter. This did not mean 3 John was any less inspired; it just took longer to gain wide acceptance.

PROJECT NUMBER 2

It is becoming obvious to us then, that the process of recognition and collection was both long and slow. In it there was a mysterious mingling of the human and divine. List as many elements as you can in each category.

The Human	The Divine

III. The Formation

Both human and divine elements combine in the formation of the New Testament canon. It was completed, of course, when the last of the inspired books was written. They were immediately authoritative by virtue of their inspiration. During the early centuries of the Church Age, however, the gradual recognition of these authoritative books can be traced. This recognition and collection developed in three major stages.[4]

A. The Early Stage A.D. 70-170, the Period of Circulation and Collection

1. THE GOSPELS AND ACTS

The collection of Matthew, Mark, Luke and Acts was almost certainly completed before A.D. 80. John's Gospel probably was written later than this date, and by A.D. 150 the fourfold Gospel canon was known.

Clement, bishop of Rome about A.D. 95, gives clear testimony to Matthew and Luke. The facts and teachings of Christ found in the Gospels occur extensively in the writings of Ignatius, bishop of Antioch (A.D. 117). Tatian's *Diatessaron* (about A.D. 170) was a harmony of the four Gospels that wove the materials into one continuous narrative. This is irrefutable testimony that these four Gospels had been recognized as authoritative over many other gospels, and therefore were collected early.

2. THE EPISTLES OF PAUL

Very early Paul's epistles were collected, accepted as authoritative and placed alongside the Old Testament.

Perhaps such a collection existed by A.D. 70. 2 Peter 3:15,16 testifies to such a collection and its recognition:

> And regard the patience of our Lord to be salvation; just as also our beloved brother Paul, according to the wisdom given him, wrote to you, as also in all his letters, speaking in them of those things, in which are some things hard to understand, which the untaught and unstable distort, as they do also the rest of the Scriptures, to their own destruction.

The heretic Marcion (about A.D. 150) accepted as his canon only ten epistles of Paul and Luke's Gospel. It has been argued that the canon must already have been fairly well defined for Marcion to react so strongly against it.

3. OTHER WRITINGS

By A.D. 170, all other New Testament books were noticed in the writings of the church fathers except 2 Peter. Only 2 Peter, 2 and 3 John seemed to be without a substantial footing in the canon. Only one extra canonical book

(Apocalypse of Peter) ran the risk of being accepted.

Therefore by A.D. 170 the books of the New Testament were widely circulated individually. Almost all of them were recognized as authoritative, primarily because of the apostolicity. They were even now being gathered in collections of authoritative books.

B. The Intermediate Stage A.D. 170-303, the Period of Confirmation and Separation

The intermediate stage covers the period of time from Tatian's *Diatessaron* to Diocletian's persecution and includes the testimony of Irenaeus, Tertullian, Origen and others.

These writers confirmed the expressed views of the early writers. They acknowledged the authority of the apostolic writings. They substantially agreed on which books were to be recognized as authoritative. The books that were not received were not rejected, but simply were little known or not known to them at all (e.g., 2 Peter, 2 and 3 John, Jude, Hebrews, James). It is during this period that the Apocrypha books virtually passed out of use. The separation between canonical books and ecclesiastical literature made in the early stage was becoming more distinct and settled in this stage.

C. The Final Stage A.D. 303-397, the Period of Final Ratification

It was in this period that the New Testament canon was formally settled. In A.D. 363 the Council of Laodicea requested that only canonical books of the Old and New Testament be read in the churches. They proceeded to enumerate these books, and listed all the books of our New Testament except Revelation.

In A.D. 367 Athanasius of Alexandria published a list of writings that were considered authoritative. Here is the first list, which included the exact thirty-nine books of the Old Testament and the twenty-seven books of the New Testament.

Jerome (A.D. 385) recognized the same New Testament collection in his translation of the Latin Vulgate.

The Council at Hippo in A.D. 393 and the Council at Carthage in A.D. 397 "officially acknowledged the canons of both Testaments, including the twenty-seven books, and forbade any others to be read in the churches."[5]

The decisions of these councils did not make the books authoritative. Rather they expressed the prevailing view of Christians. The councils simply acknowledged the authority of these writings. It was not the church that shaped the canon, rather it was the canon that shaped the church.

PROJECT NUMBER 3

From the above survey of the formation of the New Testament canon, complete

the following chart.[6]	STAGE 1	STAGE 2	STAGE 3
Date			
Period of			
Summary of its characteristics			

The preceding chart will help to summarize the details of the previous few pages. It bears testimony to the slow but certain recognition by the church of those writings inspired by God.

With this background we are ready to entertain the tantalizing question of the extent of canon, raised by my two Mormon visitors. This is not a new question. It was a problem among Christians in the early church. It divided believers in the Reformation Age. It has reared its troublesome head once again in our age. Is the Bible a complete or incomplete revelation? Is the canon closed or open? Could God give us another book that merits equal status with the sixty-six of our Bible? To be sure, the question of the extent of the canon is a thorny problem to handle—but handle it we must.

IV. The Problem

What is the extent of the canon? This is our problem. It will perhaps be most useful to segment our subject into three time periods: the early centuries, the Reformation period and the present day.

A. In The Early Centuries

The abundance of literature in the apostolic and post-apostolic ages was, in a sense, a mixed blessing. To many hundreds of believers it was the source of great blessing. As well, however, it created many problems. Which books were inspired, authentic, apostolic and authoritative? Which were not? The profusion of literature may be sorted into four classifications:

1. THE UNDISPUTED BOOKS

Twenty of the New Testament books were widely accepted within a century by all Christians. There was no dispute over their canonicity.

2. THE DISPUTED BOOKS

During the early and intermediate stages, seven books were disputed.
Revelation was highly esteemed in the churches in Asia between A.D. 100 and
180. After A.D. 200 its canonicity was disputed for two main reasons. In this
period there "was an increasing departure from the premillennial expectations
of the Early Church."[7] As this was taught most specifically in Revelation, it
raised questions about the book. The denial of the book by some was prompted by their denial of its apostolic authorship, and it was attributed to
Cerinthus or another John. This charge was not made until 100 years after its
writing, and was raised by the anti-millennarians to discredit the millennial
teaching of Revelation.

The book of *2 Peter* has little testimony to its apostolic origin in the early
centuries. However the internal evidence clearly indicates Petrine authorship
(2 Pet. 1:1; 1:14; 1:17; 3:1). It is not immediately clear why it was neglected
by the early church.

Although the external evidence for *2 and 3 John* is scanty, yet there is sufficient to indicate a definite tradition that acknowledged its apostolicity. Its
relative insignificance accounts for its limited circulation and later recognition.

The uncertainty as to the acceptance of *James* and *Jude* seems to have
resulted from the identity of the authors. Who were James and Jude? There
were two or three men with the name James and also with the name Jude. The
Roman Catholic church has concluded these men are the James and Jude listed
among the twelve apostles (Luke 6:16; and Acts 1:13). The normal Protestant
view is that these were the half brothers of our Lord (Matt. 13:55; Mark 6:3),
who later came to be believers and were considered among the apostles.
(James—1 Corinthians 15:7; Galatians 1:19. Tertullian speaks of Jude the
Apostle.) Gradually the apostolicity of the books gained recognition for them.

Hebrews was open to much discussion, due again to the problem of
authorship. The Pauline authorship that was accepted in the East by Origen
and Clement, was held in doubt in the West. Irenaeus denied Pauline authorship. Tertullian said it was written by Barnabas. "Who wrote the epistle, in
truth, God knows," wrote Origen. However, in the course of time it was
accepted, perhaps on the same basis as Luke and Mark—that is, an authorship
that was directly linked with an apostle, making the actual author something
of a secondary author.

3. THE NEW TESTAMENT APOCRYPHA

These writings come from the second to fifth centuries A.D., and were written
either to satisfy curiosity about the thirty silent years of Christ and the ministry of disciples quietly passed over in the canonical *Acts*, or to foist heretical
ideas upon the church with the alleged endorsement of Christ and His apostles. These were not apostolic in origin, were never considered as canonical by
the church fathers, and are often worthless, heretical and very fanciful with an
excess of the miraculous.

Although the details of these books will be largely unfamiliar to most of us, their names we have heard often. They may be classified according to the very four categories found in our New Testament.[8]

Gospels: The Protevangelium of James, Pseudo-Matthew, The Gospel of Thomas, The Gospel according to the Hebrews, the Gospel of Peter, the Gospel of Nicodemus, The Acts of Pilate.

Origen said, "The church receives only four gospels, heretics have many."

Acts: The Acts of Peter, The Acts of Paul, The Acts of John, The Acts of Andrew, The Acts of Thomas.

Epistles: The Epistle of the Apostles, The Epistle to the Laodiceans, The Corinthian Correspondence of Paul, Letters of Christ and Abgar, The Correspondence of Paul and Seneca.

Apocalypse: The Apocalypse of Peter, The Apocalypse of Paul.

4. THE WRITINGS OF THE POST-APOSTOLIC AGE

From the church fathers of the second, third and fourth centuries came scores of writings that were quickly and widely circulated. Although these do not claim to be Scripture, they are invaluable for their testimony to the authority of the writings of the apostles, and the recognition of the canonical books. They are known as ecclesiastical writings, but were not apostolic in origin. For this reason these writings were excluded from public worship, but were read for personal edification.

Do you recognize the names of any of these? The Epistle of Clement to Corinth, The Epistle of Barnabas, Polycarp's Epistle to the Philippians, The Didache and The Shepherd of Hermas are but a few of them.

From these four classes of literature the early church, under the providence of God and through the witness of the Spirit, recognized and collected twenty-seven books that met all the tests of inspiration. This is our New Testament. The battle, however, was far from over. The controversy of the canon was to reappear in the tumultuous sixteenth century.

B. In the Reformation Period

The attitude of the Reformers toward the extent of the canon reflects the areas of uncertainty in the early church.

Luther rejected Hebrews, James, Jude and Revelation as canonical and placed them at the end of his New Testament. He believed Hebrews contradicted Paul and his doctrine of repentance, James contradicted Romans, Jude was a copy of 2 Peter and "an unnecessary epistle to be reckoned among the chief books," and Revelation did not proclaim Christ. His followers, however, recognized all twenty-seven books as authoritative. Today we can see the weaknesses of Luther's criticisms.

Tyndale, in England, followed Luther in recognizing the disputed character of some of the books. However, all twenty-seven are included in his Bible.

Calvin omitted 2 and 3 John and Revelation from his commentary, but referred to them in his *Institutes*. He certainly accepted James and Jude, but doubted the authenticity of 2 Peter.

It is apparent then, that the reformers did not ever consider the addition of any books to the canon of the New Testament. They did doubt some of the books disputed in the early church. However, their reasons for doing so can generally be explained away today as inadequate bases for rejecting the books.

On April 8, 1546, at the Council of Trent, the Roman church accepted eleven of the fourteen Old Testament Apocrypha books into its canon as "deuterocanonical." Although they were considered to be on a secondary level, they were accepted as authoritative. In the previous chapter I have noted several reasons for rejecting this position.

C. In the Present Day

Karl Barth's view on the canon is the traditional view, which states the church can't form it, only confirm and establish it. According to him, the extent of the canon stands firmly at the line drawn by the early church.

Liberalism proposes what amounts to an "open canon" with continuous revelation. They teach us that God speaks to us now through social reforms and political movements. Radical liberalism says the Bible is not the only source of truth. Anyone can write Holy Scripture today, they say.

The Church of the Latter Day Saints proposes an addition to the canon—the Book of Mormon. Brigham Young said of the book, "Every Spirit that confesseth that Joseph (Smith) is a prophet, and that the Book of Mormon is true, is of God, and every Spirit that does not is antichrist."[9]

The founder of Christian Science, Mary Baker Eddy, wrote in 1901, "I should blush to write of *Science and Health with the Key to the Scriptures,* as I have, were it of human origin, and I apart from God, its author; but as I was only a scribe echoing the harmonies of heaven in Divine Metaphysics, I cannot be super-modest of the Christian Science textbook."[10]

Evangelicals have solidly resisted any and all modern assaults on the canon of Scripture. We confidently affirm that the canon is complete and closed. But is such a position intellectually honest? Can such a stance be supported? That was my task as I turned to answer the Mormon missionaries.

V. The Case Closed

Three lines of evidence have been marshalled and presented in defence of the evangelical perspective on the canon.

A. The Testimony of Divine Providence

Canonicity is inseparably tied to the providence of God. If God intended to reveal Himself, we can expect not only God's superintending work in the writing of Scripture, but also in the preservation, collection and recognition of those inspired books. It is inconceivable that the God who "works all things after the counsel of His will" (Eph. 1:11) and whose hand cannot be thwarted (Dan. 4:35), should allow one inspired book to escape the recognition of the church and be overlooked in the collection of the books. His continuous activity in all the affairs of humankind toward the fulfilling of His own purpose guarantees to the believer a complete canon.

But is it closed? Could there not be inspired writings subsequent to the Apostolic Age? Consider our next line of evidence.

B. The Testimony of Scripture

The evidence surely seems to imply a closed canon.

> Beloved, while I was making every effort to write you about our common salvation, I felt the necessity to write to you appealing that you contend earnestly for the faith which was once for all delivered to the saints. (Jude 3)

The "faith" is the body of Christian truth that was delivered to the saints by our Lord through the apostles. Note that Jude says it was "once for all" delivered. That is, it was completely given to the saints. What the Lord gave to the saints through the apostles was not the faith in part. It was not the beginning of a revelation with more to come in subsequent generations. It was "once for all" delivered.

Although Jude was not the last inspired book to be written, this does suggest that anything written later should harmonize doctrinally with what has already been written and taught by the apostles. We do not look for new or further revelations of truth.

David Hubbard speaks to this point when he writes, "Revelation in the biblical sense has ceased, not by petering out at the end of the apostolic period, but by coming to its glorious climax in Christ and the records of His deeds."[11]

One of the primary purposes of Scripture is to unfold and record the great plan of redemption. The close tie then between Scripture and redemption strongly implies that the canon is closed with the culmination of redemptive history in Christ.

PROJECT NUMBER 4

What does Revelation 22:18,19 contribute to a discussion on the extent of the canon?

C. The Testimony of History

A historic test of canonicity has been apostolicity. This was a test set by those closest to the scene. The passing of the apostles implies the termination of inspired writings.

Since New Testament days there has been no serious attempt to reinstate books disqualified by the church, nor to add new books to the canon. Josephus speaks for the Jewish community and their attitude to the many other writings, circulating from the fifth century B.C., to the end of the first century A.D.

> From Artaxerxes (the successor of Xerxes) until our time everything has been recorded, but has not been deemed worthy of like credit with what preceded, because the exact succession of the prophets ceased. But what faith we have placed in our own writings is evident by our conduct; for though so long a time has now passed, no one has dared to add anything to them, or to take anything from them, or to alter anything in them.[12]

The 1546 decision of the Council of Trent represented the opinion of a very small segment of people. It certainly did not represent the opinion of the believers at large. Again the attempts of Christian Science and Mormonism to add new writings to the canon does not have the support of evangelical born-again believers who are being led by the Spirit (Rom. 8:14).

PROJECT NUMBER 5

What would be your response if archaeologists unearthed a genuine lost epistle written by Paul that was addressed, for example, to the Christians in Crete?

What further revelation do we need? The Scriptures have proven themselves sufficient for the doctrine and practice of Christians for centuries.

More than being adequate, they have demonstrated their supernatural quality over and over again. The influence of this Book is unparalleled. One of countless hundreds that could be told is an old story from Scotland. Thrilling and challenging stories are told of the children of the Scottish Covenanters who stood courageously for the right, even when it meant possible death. A number of children were taken and commanded to tell where their parents were hiding or to be shot to death. In spite of the soldiers' horrible threats, not one child would tell where they were. "If you do not tell me quickly you will be shot," said the commanding officer of a firing squad. The brave children only huddled closer together and kept silent. "Make them all kneel and cover their faces," commanded the officer. "Please, sir, may I hold my brother's hand?" pleaded one little lassie. "It will make it easier for him." Others prayed. "Please, sir," said a little lad, "let us sing a song which our mothers taught us!" They began to sing, "The Lord is my shepherd, I'll not want!" Tears ran down the faces of some of the soldiers. The commanding officer himself was deeply touched. He too had learned that Psalm at his mother's knee. While the children were singing, the officer gave the command to retreat. Silently they withdrew. Their guns had been loaded only with powder, but the children didn't know that.

This Book is the living Word of God!

My interview that afternoon ended abruptly. After offering my three lines of evidence for a closed and complete canon, the younger of the two leaned forward with a deeply earnest look on his face. Briefly he told me of his concern. He had a message for me that he felt compelled to deliver and in a sentence or two summed up the "good news" of Joseph Smith.

I courteously thanked him for his interest in me, silently wondering what was so good about his news. Then I took the last minute of our time together to restate the good news of Jesus Christ: "But God demonstrates His own love toward us, in that while we were yet sinners, Christ died for us." (Rom. 5:8)

That's good news!

Review

Now is the time to turn back to the ten questions that prepared the way for this chapter. Reread them. Can you answer each question now? Take time to look up any answers that escaped you. Check your answers with the text of this chapter. Do not leave here until you have mastered the main points of the chapter.

For Further Study

1. Read the synopsis of many of the New Testament Apocrypha books in the *Introduction to the New Testament,* by Everitt F. Harrison, p.117 ff. In what specific ways are these accounts of the life of Christ in contrast with the New Testament Gospels?

2. Study carefully the history, claims and content of the Book of Mormon. In what specific areas do its teachings contradict the teachings of the Bible?

END NOTES

[1] David Hubbard, "How We Got Our New Testament," *Eternity,* February, 1971, p.14.

[2] Laird Harris, *Inspiration and Canonicity of the Bible* (Grand Rapids, MI: Zondervan Publishing House, 1969), p.237.

[3] *Ibid.,* p.236.

[4] These stages are those outlined by Dr. S.L. Johnson, Jr. (Unpublished class notes, Dallas Theological Seminary, 1967).

[5] David Hubbard, "How We Got Our New Testament," p.57.

[6] This chart is an expansion of the very useful chart by Dr. Tenney. Merrill C. Tenney, *New Testament Survey* (Grand Rapids, MI: Wm. B. Eerdmans Publishing Co., 1961), p.430.

[7] Laird Harris, *Inspiration and Canonicity of the Bible,* p.258.

[8] For details on each book see: Everett F. Harrison, *Introduction to the New Testament* (Grand Rapids, MI: Wm. B. Eerdmans Publishing Co., 1965), p.117 ff.

[9] Wm. C. Irvine, *Heresies Expanded* (New York, NY: Loizeaux Brothers, Inc., 1955), p.130.

[10] *Ibid.,* p.66.

[11] David Hubbard, "How We Got Our Bible," *Eternity,* February, 1971, p.58.

[12] Gleason Archer, *A Survey of Old Testament Introduction* (Chicago, IL: Moody Press, 1966), p.63.

BIBLIOGRAPHY

Earle, Ralph. *How We Got Our Bible.* Grand Rapids, MI: Baker Book House, 1972.

Harris, R. Laird. *Inspiration and Canonicity of the Bible.* Grand Rapids, MI: Wm. B. Eerdmans Publishing Company, 1969.

Harrison, Everett F. *Introduction to the New Testament.* Grand Rapids, MI: Wm. B. Eerdmans Publishing Company, 1965.

Henry, Carl F.H. (ed.). *Revelation and the Bible.* (Grand Rapids, MI: Baker Book House, 1967.

Metzger, Bruce M. *The Canon of the New Testament: Its Origin, Development and Significance.* Oxford University Press, 1989.

Miller, H.S. *General Biblical Introduction.* Houghton, NY: The Word—Rearer Press, 1952.

Orr, James (ed.). *The International Standard Bible Encyclopedia,* 5 vols. Grand Rapids, MI: Wm. B. Eerdmans Publishing Co., 1939.

Pinnock, Clark H. *Biblical Revelation.* Chicago, IL: Moody Press, 1971.

Van Campenhausen, Hans. *The Formation of the Christian Bible.* Philadelphia, PA: Fortress Press, 1972.

Part VI

ੴ

TEXTUAL CRITICISM

CHAPTER EIGHT

৯

CONSTRUCTIVE
CRITICISM

Preparing the Way

1. What is textual criticism?

2. How does lower criticism differ from higher criticism?

3. What are the two main problems of a textual critic?

4. How many original manuscripts of the Bible do we have today?

5. What are the two oldest complete manuscripts?

6. What is a textual variant?

7. There are 150,000 variants in the New Testament. True or false?

8. What doctrines are seriously affected by textual variations?

9. In what sense can we say that we have today the content of the original manuscripts?

10. What raging controversy in textual criticism today touches every one of us because of the influences in our translations?

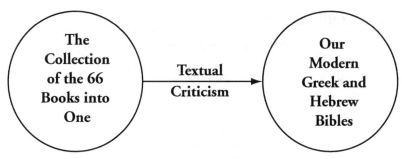

Can I really trust my Bible? I have asked myself that question a hundred times. It is very important to me personally. Before I can stake my future on its teachings, before I can commit my life to obey it, I have to know, Is it really trustworthy? As a young man this question constantly haunted me. Having no answer would leave me in a state of limbo: neutral, uncommitted, insecure and frustrated. A negative answer would hurl me into a state of reckless despair. A positive answer would give me an anchor, a rudder, a compass and a course.

I have since discovered that such a dilemma is no unique experience. It is par for the course. Most thinking and sensitive Christians sooner or later enter into that valley of decision and wrestle with the trustworthiness of their Bible. How they emerge often determines the course of their lives.

This was certainly true of Billy Graham. As a young preacher of the gospel, he fought this very same battle. He loves to tell of that moment of triumph when, by God's great grace, he quietly accepted the Bible from God as His Holy Word, to believe it, to preach it and to live it. That step of faith set the direction for his life. It turned the tide in his ministry. It has affected the nations of the earth. How we have all thrilled to his decisive and dynamic declarations, "The Bible says … ." In the final analysis, of course, every such decision is a step of faith. But faith is not blind. It is not irrational. It is always rooted in facts. Now mark this well. As never before, the facts warrant our implicit faith in the trustworthiness of our Bibles. Overwhelming evidence comes from the little-known and often misunderstood work of textual criticism. It is to this field of study that we now turn.

Since, by definition, inspiration extends only to the original manuscripts of our Bible, and since none of the original manuscripts are in existence today, how can we rely upon the accuracy of our modern Hebrew and Greek Bibles? This, of course, is an important question because the translations of our English Bibles are based upon the available Greek and Hebrew Bibles.

The science of textual criticism answers this question and bridges the gap.

If you have been in Christian circles long, you have frequently heard of the mysterious and mischievous "critics." They are an oft-maligned company of persons, enemies of the faith, opponents of the truth. Although you would be hard pressed to name even one, you have developed a hostile prejudice against them. We speak of them with disdain. We hear a silent hiss with any reference to these critics in public. The very mention of their names causes us to bristle with indignation. You may not be entirely fair. In fact, you may be completely wrong.

I. An Identity Crisis

Some critics are your best friends. You are deeply indebted to them. They have immeasurably enriched your life. They offer invaluable service to you.

Meet, please, a textual critic. This scholar spends hundreds of lone, long hours poring over ancient parchments, dating, translating, classifying and comparing them. By applying certain principles to the manuscripts, the critic strives to determine the original inspired writing. How thankful to God we must be for these dedicated and godly men and women who have left us with such a heritage. To be sure, they are critics. But do not divest them of their identity. He or she is a textual critic who is devoted to the science of textual criticism.

Textual criticism is simply the work of scholars with the available manuscripts aimed at recovering, as nearly as possible, the original text. This distinguishes textual criticism from the other major area of criticism: higher criticism. Textual criticism, sometimes called *lower criticism*, is concerned only with the text of Scripture itself and is aimed at finding the true text as it came from the author. On the other hand, *higher criticism* is concerned with matters outside the text such as the date of writing, integrity, historicity, etc. It is from this breed of critic that the most withering attacks against Scripture have come. Negative, liberal, higher criticism is the camp of the enemy.

PROJECT NUMBER 1

1. Construct your own chart of contrasts and comparisons between the two schools of critics.

Higher Criticism	Lower Criticism

2. Name three prominent critics in each field of criticism.

Our interest in this chapter is not in the higher critic, but in the lower critic, the textual critic. This critic has served us well. And yet the work has not been easy.

II. A Double Distress

The textual critic in every age has faced two major problems. Initially they appear insurmountable. To many Christians, uninitiated into the problems of the text, they at first are very disturbing. Opponents of the Scriptures constantly revert to them for ammunition in their assaults on the reliability of the Bible. We must know and understand both problems if we ever are to be able to give an answer to an anxious enquirer, or to contend earnestly for the faith with an antagonist. It will surely go a long way toward establishing your faith and confirming you in it too. Now, what are these two problems?

A. The Problem of No Original Manuscripts

As a matter of fact, the situation is even worse than this. The earliest complete extant Hebrew manuscript is dated at the eleventh century A.D. That is fourteen centuries after the closing of the Old Testament canon! Here are fourteen hundred years of constant copying by hand, fourteen hundred years for errors to creep into our manuscripts.

The situation is somewhat better in the case of the Greek manuscripts of the New Testament. The earliest complete extant manuscript in this category is dated at A.D. 350. Once again, however, we have 250–300 years of copying, often under the poorest of circumstances. Imagine the potential for errors to creep into the text.

Does this disturb you? We cannot ignore it. These are the facts. Now we can see the imperative for textual criticism. How this helps us appreciate the immense task of the textual critics. They are seeking to hurdle several silent centuries to recover for us the original text.

I have had this problem hurled at me dozens of times by college students, businessmen, skeptics and atheists. Some are serious seekers, others are vocal opponents. Their charge cannot be quickly dismissed. We claim to have an inerrant authoritative word from God on matters of creed and conduct, yet we have no original manuscripts of the word and there are actually hundreds of years between the alleged original and the extant manuscripts. This cannot be simply ignored.

In answer to the problem of no original manuscripts three points must be made.

First, there are no original manuscripts available for any writings of antiquity. Did you realize this? We have not one original manuscript of the writings of Homer, Plato, Aristotle, Seneca, Cicero or any other writer of antiquity.

Author	Writing	Date	No. of Manuscripts	Years between Original & Extant
Caesar	Gallic War	58-50 B.C.	9-10 good	900
Tacitus	History, 14 books	A.D. 100	4?	800-1000
Tacitus	Annals, 16 books	A.D. 100	10	800-1000
Thucydides	History	460-400 B.C.	8	1300

After surveying this evidence, F.F. Bruce concludes:

> Yet no classical scholar would listen to an argument that the
> authenticity of Herodotus or Thucydides is in doubt because
> the earliest manuscripts of their works which are of any use
> to us are over 1,300 years later than the originals.[1]

We do not need to be apologetic about the Bible. No piece of ancient literature can make the claim of an extant original.

Second, there are significant parts of both the Old and New Testament dated many centuries earlier than the first complete manuscript. The John Rollins papyrus of John 18:31-33 and 37-38 is probably the earliest fragment of any part of the New Testament. It dates back to A.D. 140.

Third, there is a vast abundance of biblical manuscripts available to us today for our study. There are more than 5,300 Greek manuscripts of the New Testament alone. Think of it. In addition to these, the textual critic has thousands of versions: 8,000 of the Latin Vulgate and another 1,000 of early translations into Egyptian, Syrian, etc. Add to these the many quotations from the New Testament in the writings of the church fathers of the first two centuries. It is estimated that much of the New Testament could be reproduced from the quotations of these early fathers alone. Still more early information is available from the lectionaries—the reading lessons in public church services.

Sir Fredric Kenyon, a world-renowned scholar in this field says:

> The interval then, between the dates of original composition
> and the earliest extant evidence, becomes so small as to be in
> fact, negligible, and the last foundation for any doubt that
> the Scriptures have come down to us substantially as they
> were written has now been removed. Both the authenticity
> and the general integrity of the books of the New Testament
> may be regarded as finally established.[2]

It is clearly apparent then, to any careful reader that no writing of the ancient world is nearly as well-documented bibliographically as the New Testament. The problem of no original manuscripts is no problem to the average Christian today. It remains a problem for the textual critic alone, and thanks to the abundance of early manuscripts that problem can be virtually eliminated. But what about the other problem?

B. The Problem of Errors

Because the printing press was not invented until the fifteenth century, the early copies of the manuscripts were made by scribes, professional copiers. In the process however, many errors were made by these scribes. Some were unintentional, others were intentional. Whatever, they are a major problem for the textual critic. Perhaps it will help you appreciate their problem if we pause for a moment to consider how these errors crept into the copied manuscripts.

First, some errors were unintentional. There were errors of sight when a scribe would skip a line or a phrase, or would confuse letters that were similar in form. After the fourth century the scriptorium emerged—a room where scribes sat at desks copying a manuscript that was dictated to them. Errors of hearing crept into the text as the scribes misunderstood words that sounded alike. Often there were errors of the mind as well. A lapse of concentration between hearing or reading and recording what they heard or read, resulted in reversed word order, transposed letters and even substituted synonyms. All such errors were unintentional, of course. They must be attributed to the frailty of the flesh. Not so, however, with the second category.

Second, other errors were intentionally made by conscientious and pious scribes who had nothing but the best of intentions. Sometimes they were attempting to harmonize parallel passages such as the Gospel accounts of identical events. For example, we know one scribe added "It was written in Hebrew, Latin and Greek" to his copy of Luke 23:38 to make it agree with John 19:20. In other instances intentional changes were made in grammar to correct what the scribe supposed was a grammatical error (see Revelation 1:4). Occasionally changes were made for theological purposes. One scribe left "neither the Son" out of his copy of Mark 13:32 because it appeared to him that to say even the Son did not know the day of His coming was to deny the deity of Christ. Such errors were made intentionally by scribes with the highest of motives.

PROJECT NUMBER 3

Consider the variants in the following texts. Is it intentional or unintentional? Into which sub-category does each one fall?

Revelation 1:5—to loose or to wash.

1 Corinthians 6:20—the last phrase of the verse.

John 19:14—some manuscripts read the "third" hour.

Acts 9:5,6 and 26:14,15—See the KJV and NASB.

Now, note this very carefully. Strictly speaking, such changes in the copies are not errors. They are *variants*—variations that have crept into copies of manuscripts. There are about 150,000 textual variants or various readings! The work of the textual critic is to identify the variants and to recover the original reading.

Lest we misunderstand, however, and discredit the work of the scribes, we must consider the extreme care of these ancient copies. They so reverenced the text of Scripture that they went to unbelievable lengths to preserve its exact words. They actually counted not only the words but every letter in the Old Testament and made records as to where and how often each letter was found.

Sidney Collett helpfully points out the care that was taken:

> Moreover, each new copy has to be made from an approved
> manuscript, written with a special kind of ink, upon sheets
> made from the skin of a "clean" animal. The writers also had
> to pronounce aloud each word before writing it, and on no
> account was a single word to be written from memory. They
> were to reverently wipe their pen before writing the name of
> God in any form, and to wash their whole body before writ-
> ing "Jehovah," lest that holy name should be tainted even in
> the writing. The new copy was then carefully examined with
> the original almost immediately; and it is said that if only one
> incorrect letter were discovered the whole copy was rejected!

> The Rev. J.P. Smyth tells how one rabbi solemnly warned a
> scribe thus, "Take heed how thou doest thy work, for thy
> work is the work of heaven, lest thou drop or add a letter of
> the manuscript, and so become a destroyer of the world!"[3]

One check on the accuracy of the New Testament manuscripts was by
means of measuring the number of lines in a manuscript. Bruce Metzger
points out that several manuscripts speak of 2,560, 1,616, 2,750 and 2,024
lines respectively for the four Gospels. This, by the way, implies the presence
of Mark 16:9-20, and the absence of John 7:53-8:11, in those writings.[4]

In the scriptoria of the monasteries, certain rules and penalties were
enforced to secure a high degree of accuracy in copying. Somewhere I came
across the following example of such regulations prepared for the renowned
monastery of the Stadium at Constantinople.

> About A.D. 800, the abbot of this monastery, Theodore the
> Studite, who was himself highly skilled in writing an elegant
> Greek hand, included in his rules for the monastery severe
> punishments for monks who were not careful in copying
> manuscripts. A diet of bread and water was the penalty set for
> the scribe who became so much interested in the subject mat-
> ter of what he was copying that he neglected his task of copy-
> ing. Monks had to keep their parchment leaves neat and
> clean, on penalty of 130 penances. If anyone should take
> without permission another's quaternion (that is, the ruled
> and folded sheets of parchment), fifty penances were pre-
> scribed. If anyone should make more glue than he could use
> at one time, and it should harden, he must do fifty penances.
> If a scribe broke his pen in a fit of temper (perhaps after hav-
> ing made some accidental blunder near the close of an other-
> wise perfectly copied sheet), he had to do thirty penances.

In spite of such dedication and discipline, "errors" or variants did creep into the manuscripts as they were copied by hand before the days of the printing press.

Here is the double distress of the textual critic. There are no original manuscripts and there are 150,000 New Testament textual variants. It is toward resolving the difficulties raised by these problems that the textual critics devote their scholarly lives. How effective have they been?

III. The Results

The results of textual criticism are most helpful. Thanks to copyists' diligent work and God's providence in making available so many manuscripts, their variants can be easily detected and, as a rule, corrected by the reading of other manuscripts.

While the number of various readings is large, and therefore disturbing to many Christians, the facts are really very reassuring.

Of the 150,000 various readings, we are now able to discuss nineteen-twentieths. No textual critic regards them as having any serious claim to reception. This leaves us with about 7,500.

Nineteen out of twenty of these remaining variations are matters of word order, grammar and spelling. They do not concern the meaning of the text in any way.

Now we have remaining about 400 variations. Sometimes it is omission or addition of words. They make no difference in the meaning of the text, and are the objects of curiosity and interest. A very few exceptional cases may be considered important.

In dealing with the majority of these exceptional areas, we have such an abundance of excellent critical helps that textual critics are able to determine the original and true text with a high degree of confidence.

Philip Schaff, in *Companion to the Greek Testament and the English Version,* concluded that only 400 of the 150,000 caused doubt about the textual meaning and only 50 of these were of great significance. Not one of the variations, Schaff says, altered "an article of faith or a precept of duty which is not abundantly sustained by other and undoubted passages, or by the whole tenor of Scripture teaching."[5]

Geisler and Nix say, concerning the observation of F.J.A. Hort:

> Only about one-eighth of all the variants had any weight, as most of them are merely mechanical matters such as spelling or style. Of the whole then, only about one-sixtieth rise above "trivialities," or can in any sense be called "substantial variations." Mathematically this would compute to a text that is 98.33 percent pure.[6]

F.J.A. Hort says that apart from insignificant variations of grammar or spelling, not more than one thousandth part of the New Testament is affected by differences of reading.[7]

These witnesses adamantly affirm the reliability of our Greek New Testament text. The same can be said for our Old Testament text. Paul Little wrote:

> In 1947, the world learned about what has been called the greatest archeological discovery of the century. In caves, in the valley of the Dead Sea, ancient jars were discovered containing the now famous Dead Sea Scrolls. From these scrolls, it is evident that a group of Jews lived at a place called Qumran from about 150 B.C. to A.D. 70. Theirs was a communal society, operated very much like a monastery. In addition to tilling the fields, they spent their time studying and copying the Scriptures. It became apparent to them that the Romans were going to invade the land. They put their leather scrolls in jars and hid them in caves in the side of the cliffs west of the Dead Sea.
>
> In the providence of God, the scrolls survived undisturbed until discovered accidentally by a wandering Bedouin goat herdsman in February or March of 1947. The accidental discovery was followed by careful exploration, and several other caves containing scrolls have been located. The find included the earliest manuscript copy yet known of the complete book of Isaiah, and fragments of almost every book in the Old Testament. In addition, there is a fragmented copy containing much of Isaiah 38-66. The books of Samuel, in a tattered copy, were also found, along with two complete chapters of Habakkuk. A number of nonbiblical items, including the rules of the ancient community, were also discovered.
>
> The significance of this find, for those who wonder about the accuracy of the Old Testament text, can easily be seen. In one dramatic stroke, almost 1,000 years were hurdled in terms of the age of the manuscripts we now possess. By comparing the Dead Sea Scrolls with the Massoretic text, we would get a clear indication of the accuracy, or lack of it, of transmission over the period of nearly a millennium.[8]

What was actually learned? In comparing the Qumran manuscripts of Isaiah 38-66 with the one we had, scholars found that "the text is extremely close to our Massoretic text. A comparison of Isaiah 53 shows that only 17 letters differ from the Massoretic text. Ten of these are mere differences of spelling, like our "honor" or "honour," and produce no change in the meaning at all. Four more are very minor differences, such as the presence of a conjunction, which is often a matter of style. The other three letters are the Hebrew word for "light" which is added after "they shall see" in verse 11. Out of 166 words in this chapter, only this one word is really in question, and it does not at all change the sense of the passage. This is typical of the whole manuscript."[9]

This is but a sample of the evidence that could be marshalled in defence of the reliability of our Old Testament Hebrew manuscripts.

Therefore, for all practical purposes, although we do not have the original manuscripts, we can say that we have the *content* of the original manuscripts in our modern Hebrew and Greek Bibles.

It is surely obvious, then, that in spite of having no original manuscripts and of having many variants in our available manuscripts, the substance of our Bible is very reliable. As with no other book of antiquity there is an abundance of manuscripts, translations and quotations from which our textual critics are able to affirm the content of the originals.

Although we have considered the two primary problems encountered in textual criticism, today there still remains however, lurking in the shadows, a third problem. A brief exposure to it here will pave the way for our study of translations in the upcoming chapter.

IV. A Raging Controversy

A short time ago a devout evangelical pastor stepped into his pulpit to announce to his Sunday morning congregation that the only Bible to be used in the teaching of their church was the King James Version. His proclamation sent a shock wave through the crowd.

Last year a friend of mine candidating for a ministry in a mid-west evangelical church, was rejected because he used a modern version of the Scriptures in his preaching.

While speaking at a Bible conference a year or two ago, a humble and faithful servant of the Lord poured out his broken heart to me. He had just been called a heretic. The charge? He was using a modern translation. His accuser was a loyal supporter of the King James Version who had launched a crusade in their church that threatened its very unity.

What is all the fuss about anyway?

Simply stated, the debate is between the oldest Greek texts and the majority Greek texts. The majority text is the Greek text found in the host of later manuscripts that formed the basis of Erasmus's Greek New Testament, and ultimately the King James Version. Since the publication of the Authorized Version in A.D. 1611, some much older manuscripts have been discovered, notably codex Sinaiticus and codex Vaticanus, both of the fourth century. In addition, papyri of the New Testament have been discovered that are dated in the third century. The differences between the Received Text, which formed the basis of the Authorized Version, and the older manuscripts has erupted into a controversy—in some circles, a very heated controversy.

The question is this, Which text is the better text, the more reliable and authentic text—the majority text or the older text? The overwhelming opinion of scholarship today is in favour of the older text.[10] The oldest manuscripts are today commonly classified as "the best manuscripts."

The discovery of many older manuscripts, and the above conclusion of textual criticism, have led to many revisions of the English Bible. Some of the changes in the text and explanatory notes in the margin of these revisions become intelligible only upon understanding this controversy in textual criticism. It may be of help to consider one or two examples.

> For there are three that bear record in heaven, the Father, the Word, and the Holy Ghost: and these three are one. (1 John 5:7 AV)

Yet this great "trinitarian witness," as it is frequently called, is omitted entirely from the New American Standard Bible and most other modern translations. Why? Because there is no support for it whatsoever from the older manuscripts. Actually the oldest witness to it comes from a Latin treatise of the fourth century. It does not appear in the Vulgate until after A.D. 800. It was not included in the first and second edition of Erasmus's New Testament (1516, 1519) because he said there was no Greek witness whatsoever for its support. In the midst of protests, Erasmus promised to include it in his next edition if he could find one Greek witness. A manuscript appeared in 1520, and Erasmus was compelled to include it in his third edition (1522) with the footnote that he believed the manuscript had been expressly prepared to confute him. From this third edition of Erasmus, it found its place in the Received Text and the Authorized Version. But where was the support? Older manuscripts recently discovered have confirmed it to be unauthentic. It is therefore omitted from the text of most revised versions. This in no way affects the doctrine, of course. The truth of the Trinity rests upon the broad foundation of both the Old and New Testament (Gen. 1:26; Isa. 9:6; Matt. 28:18-20; John 10:30, etc.).

Consider a second example:

> For an angel went down at a certain season into the pool, and troubled the water; whosoever then first after the troubling of the water stepped in was made whole of whatsoever disease he had. (John 5:4 AV)

Yet, once again, this verse is omitted from the text of the New American Standard Bible and most modern translations. Why? It is not found in the older and "better" manuscripts. It is missing from two early papyri, P66 (about A.D. 200) and P75 (early third century), and from both codex

Viticanus and codex Sinaiticus of the fourth century.

In all likelihood this verse originally was an explanatory note placed by some scribe in the margin of his manuscript. In the course of time it was eventually incorporated into the text itself as a helpful explanation of the incident. But there is no evidence from the earliest manuscripts that it was part of the original text. For this reason it is omitted from the modern translations, which are based upon the older manuscripts. It is this kind of thing that has unsettled many Christians, and occasioned many attacks against newer translations. The controversy is a matter of textual criticism.

PROJECT NUMBER 4

1. What is the textual problem in Acts 8:37? How do you explain this problem?

2. Consider carefully the textual problem of Mark 16:9-20. What is the problem? How do you explain it?

Can I really trust my Bible? According to our textual critics: absolutely. They offer reassurance upon reassurance. How grateful to God we must be for the contributions of such scholars. And yet, you might protest, their product is the Greek and Hebrew Bible. Ours is the English Bible. Can the same thing be said for it? Just how reliable is it? Can I hold it in my hand and point to it as the Word of God? This question drives us to the next stage in the process. It takes us beyond the work of textual criticism to the science of translation.

FOR FURTHER STUDY

Prepare a concise book review of *Which Bible?* *by* David Otis Fuller. (Grand Rapids, MI: Grand Rapids International Publications, 1971). Fuller argues in support of the Received Text—the King James Version. How would you evaluate his case?

End Notes

[1] F.F. Bruce, *Are the New Testament Documents Reliable?* (London: The InterVarsity Fellowship, 1950), pp.16,17.

[2] Sir Fredric Kenyon, *The Bible and Archaeology* (New York, NY: Harper and Row, 1940), pp.288,289.

[3] Sidney Collett, *All About the Bible* (Westwood, NJ: Fleming H. Revell Company, 1959), p.15.

[4] Bruce Metzger, *The Text of the New Testament* (New York, NY: Oxford University Press, 1968), p.16.

[5] Philip Schaff, *A Companion to the Greek Testament and the English Version* (London: MacMillan and Co., 1883), p.177.

[6] Norman L. Geisler and William E. Nix, *A General Introduction to the Bible* (Chicago, IL: Moody Press, 1968), p.365.

[7] B.F. Westcott and F.J.A. Hort (eds.), *New Testament in Original Greek* (London: MacMillan and Company, 1881), Vol. II, p.2.

[8] Paul E. Little, *Know Why You Believe* (Wheaton, IL: Scripture Press Publications, 1967), pp.41.42.

[9] Laird R. Harris, *How Reliable Is the Old Testament Text? Can I Trust My Bible?* (Chicago, IL: Moody Press, 1963), p.124.

[10] Bruce Metzger, *The Text of the New Testament*, pp.124-146.

Bibliography

Bruce, F.F. *Are the New Testament Documents Reliable?* London: The InterVarsity Fellowship, 1950.

Collett, Sidney. *All About the Bible.* Westwood, NJ: Fleming H. Revell Company, 1959.

Fuller, David Otis. *Which Bible?* Grand Rapids, MI: Grand Rapids International Publications, 1971.

Fuller, David Otis (ed.). *True or False?* Grand Rapids, MI: Grand Rapids International Publications, 1973.

Geisler, Norman L. and Nix, William E. *A General Introduction to the Bible.* Chicago, IL: Moody Press, 1968.

Harris, Laird R. *How Reliable Is the Old Testament Text? Can I Trust My Bible?* Chicago, IL: Moody Press, 1963.

Kenyon, Sir Fredric. *The Bible and Archaeology.* New York, NY: Harper and Row, 1940.

Little, Paul E. *Know Why You Believe.* Wheaton, IL: Scripture Press Publications, Inc., 1968.

Metzger, Bruce. *The Text of the New Testament.* New York, NY: Oxford University Press, 1968.

Robertson, A.T. *An Introduction to the Textual Criticism of the New Testament.* New York, NY: Harper and Brothers Publishers, 1928.

Schaff, Philip. *Companion to the Greek Testament and the English Version,* R.N. New York, NY: Harper Brothers, 1883

Warfield, Benjamin B. *An Introduction to the Textual Criticism of the New Testament.* London: Hodder and Stoughton, 1886.

Westcott, B.F. and Hort, F. J. A. (eds.). *New Testament in Original Greek,* London: MacMillan and Company, 1881.

Part VII

و

TRANSLATION

CHAPTER NINE

৯

WHICH BIBLE?

Preparing the Way

1. Who was the translator of the first English Bible?

2. What was the occasion for the translation of the King James Version?

3. How do you account for the incredible number of modern English translations that have appeared in the twentieth century?

4. Is there any particular value in having multiple translations, or do they only cause confusion?

5. In that our English Bible is only a translation, a translation based upon manuscripts that are not even originals, dare we speak of it as the Word of God?

6. List several criteria for a good translation.

7. What is the general guideline for choosing which English Bible to use?

8. Evaluate the New American Standard Bible, The Living Bible and the New Inter-national Version.

9. Which modern English Bibles are best suited for study, and which for devotional reading?

10. Which English Bible would be most appropriate to offer to your unbelieving business associate who has just begun to show some interest in reading the Bible?

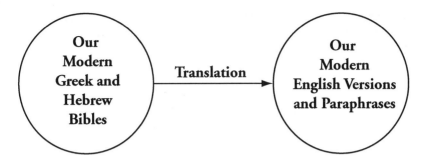

Although it is hard to believe, it is a fact that in the twentieth century alone more than one hundred and thirty English versions of all or part of the Bible have appeared in print.[1]

For some this creates a dilemma. For others it is pure delight.

Recently at a mid-week service we were presenting and comparing several of the more common translations on the market today. In our question period one of my good friends expressed the frustration of thousands when he told us how difficult he found it to follow a Scripture reading or a speaker when a different translation was being used. Wouldn't it be better to standardize and all use the same one?

It was quickly apparent that many shared his sentiments. But not all. One of the elders quietly offered his experience. He found it particularly helpful to hear or follow in another version. So there is the problem. What is depreciated by some is appreciated by others. How shall we resolve the problem? Must it be resolved? What should be our attitude toward the multiplicity of translations today? Is it a curse or a blessing?

But that is not all. There is another side to the problem. Since inspiration extends only to the original manuscripts, which are unavailable to us, and since textual criticism applies to our modern Greek and Hebrew Bibles, which few of us can read, how reliable is our English Bible today? Can we honestly speak of it as the Word of God? Which version is actually the best one? Which one should I be reading?

A study of the science of translation will help to answer these questions. It will bridge the gap between the ancient languages and our modern one. Hopefully it will help to settle the dust in our dilemma.

I. Three Milestones

A.D. 1384—It really began with John Wycliffe, a great man of God often called "the morning star of the Reformation." Because of his deep and earnest concern for the spiritual welfare of the common people he sent out poor priests, called Lollards, to preach to the people of England in their own language. At that time all preaching in the churches was in Latin, the language of the Vulgate Bible but hardly the language of the people. Wycliffe soon realized that a Bible in English was desperately needed if the common people were to hear the Gospel and read the Scriptures. Under his leadership the first English translation of the entire Bible was made from Latin in A.D. 1384.

A.D. 1525—After the interval of a century and a half, the need for a revision of Wycliffe's Bible became imperative. Because church authorities in England prohibited any new English translations, William Tyndale was forced to go to Germany, where he translated the New Testament from the original Greek for the people of his generation. In A.D. 1525 the first English New Testament was published on the printing press. Copies were smuggled into England in sacks of grain and bales of cloth. Parts of the Old Testament were also translated by Tyndale before he was betrayed, strangled and burned near Brussels.

A.D. 1611—It was the many arguments that arose from the several English versions of the seventeenth century that prompted King James I to appoint fifty-four scholars to make a new version. It took about seven years to produce. Some known copies of older manuscripts, as well as some recent translations, were consulted. The primary source however, was the Greek text of Erasmus, which was based on a handful of late and haphazardly collected manuscripts. The translation was authorized by the king himself as the standard English Bible. It was first published in A.D. 1611, and became the most popular English Bible. For two hundred and fifty years it was regarded supreme among English Bibles.

However, the past century has been one of constant challenge to the supremacy of the King James Version. The twentieth century saw more than one hundred and thirty new English translations of all or part of the Bible. This remarkable phenomenon is explained by at least four factors.

First, during the past century a vast number of earlier manuscripts became available. This gave rise to the controversy in textual criticism discussed in the previous chapter. Translators have at their disposal today hundreds of manuscripts that were unavailable in the seventeenth century, and many of them are much older and closer to the originals.

Second, thanks to the work of archaeologists, our knowledge of customs, history, geography and word meanings has increased by leaps and bounds in the last century. You can imagine how that calls for revisions and translations that reflect the fine details and differences uncovered by these scientists.

Third, the science of textual criticism as well has made significant advances.

Fourth, it should be apparent to all that languages change over the course of a century. Take, for example, the change in the meaning of "gay" just in the span of our generation. Such changes alone have demanded the revision of the English Bible for the people of this generation.

These are the four major factors that account for the incredible avalanche of twentieth century English translations.

PROJECT NUMBER 1
Draw up a list of the strengths and a list of the weaknesses of the King James Version.

Strengths	Weaknesses

II. Dilemma or Delight?

Who has not felt frustrated by the unending variety of translations? Yet this very variety offers us a greater opportunity to grasp the original meaning of the text than was given to most generations before us. One scholar may have slightly exaggerated the case when he said an English reader could ascertain 99.5 percent of the meaning of the original text by a careful reading of a good paraphrase in conjunction with two good translations. However, his emphasis is well taken. The use of several reliable translations for comparison and contrast is of the greatest value to the student of the English Bible today. Do not despise them. Rather use them. It will be to your own personal profit.

III. An Important Question

Dare we hold up an English Bible and boldly declare that this is the Word of God? You have surely seen it often done. Is this not somewhat presumptuous and ill advised? After all, it is not the original! It is not even in the language of the original. It is a translation. It may even be a poor translation of the Scriptures. Can we speak of it as the Word of God?

If our Lord and the apostles did, why can't we? Yes, that's correct—the Lord and the apostles did! They most frequently quoted from the Septuagint when they quoted the Old Testament. You will recall that the Septuagint was a Greek translation, even a rather poor translation of the Hebrew Old Testament. When our Lord and the apostles quote it, they quote it as Scripture and preface their quotations with such astounding claims that it is clear they regarded it as the Word of God. If they could so address the Septuagint, we are surely at liberty to label the King James Version or the New American Standard Bible as the Word of God. We need never hesitate to speak of our English translations as Scripture—the Word of God.

This does not mean, of course, that all translations are of equal quality and worth. This is hardly the case.

IV. A Fourfold Test

In sorting out the scores of Bibles on the market today it will be particularly useful to observe carefully four critical criteria.

First: The manuscript source. Is this simply a revision of an English translation (e.g., The Living Bible), or is it a translation from the original languages (e.g., New American Standard Bible or New International Version)? If it is indeed a translation from the Greek and Hebrew manuscripts, were the best possible and available manuscripts used by the translators? Have they used the oldest and most reliable manuscripts as their basis? This can often be determined by simply reading the preface to these Bibles.

Second: The theological perspective of the translators. This becomes of great importance when you realize that every translation involves interpretation. It is impossible to translate from one language into any other without embarking on interpretation. Because this is so, a translation by conservative and evangelical scholars is certainly to be preferred. The greater our confidence in the scholars, the greater will be our confidence in their product.

Third: The presentation of the person and work of Christ. Whenever a new translation comes to my desk I immediately check it out on this point. Carefully I read and reread the great Christological chapters of our New Testament—John 1:1-18, Philippians 2:1-11, Colossians 1 and Hebrews 1. The person and work of Christ form the touchstone of Christianity. Any translation that is to be respected by Christians must achieve a high level of reverence and accuracy in these central chapters.

Fourth: The readability of the translation. After all, that's what we want it for. That is why we are giving it as a gift to a friend. It is to be read. If it is not easy to read, if it is not appealing, inviting, expressive and communicative, then it is of little value to most people. Does it flow? To be read, it must be readable.

PROJECT NUMBER 2

Do a comparative study of the translation of Philippians 2:5-8 in several versions of the Bible.

Recently Gerald Hawthorne of Wheaton College offered some convictions regarding translations in general that are worth repeating. There were five of them.

> First, there is no perfect, inspired, best or final translation.
>
> Second, few translators deliberately distort the message of the Bible by setting forth a particular theological viewpoint.
>
> Third, every translation is to some degree an interpretation.
>
> Fourth, extremely hard work has gone into translating the Bible not to enrich the translators, but to enrich the reader.

And finally, all translations worthy of use must meet three criteria: they must be based on the best manuscripts available, include the abundance of new information on Hebrew and Greek vocabulary, and be accurate.[2]

This still leaves us with a big question.

V. Which One?

The general guideline is well stated by Hawthorne: "Let the purpose for which you are reading the Bible determine which translation you use."[3]

The Christian with several translations is very much like the carpenter with various saws, the artist with a variety of brushes, the mechanic with many wrenches or the homemaker with a dozen different salad moulds. In each case the choice of instrument is determined by the particular purpose of the worker. A variety is not only desirable, but actually essential due to the wide range of uses in each field. Imagine an electrician with only one all-purpose screwdriver. How impractical. No less practical, however, than the Christian confining oneself to only one translation when there is available a wide selection with individualistic purposes. The principle then is clear: choose your translation according to your purpose.

Let us discuss some of our more common purposes and recommend the translations most appropriate for each category. For the sake of simplicity we will not distinguish between paraphrases and translations in our discussion. To be sure, this is not an exhaustive or complete listing. It is very selective. Hopefully it will be a start.

A. For Careful Study

THE NEW AMERICAN STANDARD BIBLE (NASB), 1972

Many consider this version the closest we have to the Hebrew and Greek text. It is very literal in its translation, perhaps too literal at times to grasp the exact meaning. The stilted and unidiomatic styles make it somewhat unsuitable for pulpit use. Often smoothness and flow are sacrificed for literalness. However, for the student this proves useful over and over again.

Recently the Lockman Foundation published the New American Standard Bible update. The editorial board's purpose in making this translation was to adhere as closely as possible to the original languages of the Holy Scriptures and to make the translation in a fluent and readable style according to modern English usage.

THE NEW KING JAMES VERSION (NKJV), 1983

Preserving the flow and style of the Authorized Version of 1611, and reflecting the majority of original manuscripts, this translation maintains a majestic and reverent style while integrating present-day vocabulary and grammar.

THE NEW SCOFIELD REFERENCE BIBLE, 1967

Although the text is that of the Authorized Version, many changes have been made in the text that are very helpful to the student. With its introductions, annotations and subject chain reference, this has become the standard study Bible of dispensationalists. It contains a wealth of valuable information for anyone who cares to study the Bible carefully.

THE NEW OPEN BIBLE, 1990

The text of this study Bible is that of the New King James Version. It contains all the features of the Open Bible (such as The Christian's Guide to the New Life, visual survey of the Bible and special study aids) plus 198 pages of new features.

THE RYRIE STUDY BIBLE, 1976

This is available in the King James Version, the New American Standard and the New International Version; it contains annotated notes throughout the Old and New Testament as well as a harmony of the Gospels, a synopsis of Bible doctrine, topical and subject indexes, concordance, several topical essays and much more.

B. For Devotional Reading

The Revised Standard Version (RSV), 1952

The New English Bible (NEB), 1970

The Jerusalem Bible, 1966

Today's English Version (TEV), 1976

These are among the best of the less literal translations today. They are meaning-for-meaning rather than word-for-word in their rendering of the original manuscripts, and are excellent complements to the above study Bibles. The TEV is particularly attractive to some because of its limited vocabulary and simple style.

THE ONE YEAR BIBLE, 1985

Available in various translations, it is a wonderful arrangement of the Scriptures that enables one to read through the Bible in one year. Each day one reads a portion from the Old Testament, New Testament, Psalms and Proverbs.

THE MESSAGE, 1993

It is the New Testament in contemporary English by Eugene Peterson, published by Navpress. During this past year my wife and I have been refreshed and blessed reading together through this wonderful presentation of the Scriptures.

C. For Not-Yet Christians

THE NEW LIVING BIBLE, 1997

This is the most recent edition of The Living Bible, unquestionably the most popular edition of the Bible on the market today. Its style and vocabulary are very appealing to the casual reader of the Bible, and the message of the Gospel is clearly presented. If I were attempting to interest my neighbour or business associate in reading the Bible, I would begin with this one.

TODAY'S ENGLISH VERSION, 1976

You may prefer to use Today's English Version, with its easy vocabulary and style. The word list at the back of the edition, explaining many terms used in the text, is an attractive feature. Some feel this version is a superb example of meaning-for-meaning translation.

THE NEW TESTAMENT IN MODERN ENGLISH, 1972

This paraphrase by J.B. Phillips is also worthy of our careful scrutiny. It is perhaps the best idiomatic paraphrase available today and is invaluable not only to give to those who are not yet Christians, but to complement the study Bibles of the serious student.

D. For Children and Families

Holman's Illustrated edition of The Living Bible

Children's edition of the New International Version

The New Testament, 1975

Psalty's Kid's Bible, 1991

Adventure Bible, 1989

E. For Home Bible Classes

With not-yet Christians:
The New Living Bible
Today's English Version
New International Version

With mature Christians: Encourage the use of as many different translations as possible for the purpose of comparison.

F. For an All-Purpose Bible

Is there such a book? The New International Version has all the earmarks of such a book. It is more readable than the NASB, yet more reliable than many of the freer translations.

The quality and future of the NIV is correctly assessed by Sakae Kubo and Walter Specht when they write:

> On the whole, one must say that the NIV translation is accurate and clear. It does not have the color or striking characteristics of Phillips or the NEB, but it is dependable and straightforward. It is more modern than the RSV and less free than the NEB or Phillips. It will probably be used widely as the Bible for conservative Christians.[4]

G. For the Computer Age

The NET Bible, also known as the New English Translation, is the first of a new generation of Bible translations specifically designed to take advantage of computer and Internet technologies. This translation is now available free of charge for individual use, and can be downloaded from the Internet (www.netbible.org).

It strives for accuracy and readability, and contains thousands of notes, both for scholars and for other students of the Scriptures. It is accessible to those who may not be able to read or acquire the Bible otherwise (e.g., in China). The publishers are seeking review and criticism by scholars worldwide. Any corrections or improvements can be quickly implemented. The potential uses for such translations employing cutting edge technology are almost unlimited.

Different versions of the Bible are specifically designed to serve various purposes. How unfair it is to judge any version without ascertaining first its intended purpose. The preface of each of these versions will generally state the translators' purpose for their work. Read it carefully. Resist the temptation to judge every version on the same basis. Evaluate it in view of its intended purpose. Then use it for that purpose in your life and ministry.

Review

To reap the full dividends of your investment in reading and studying this chapter you must pause before you press forward. Don't charge into the next chapter until you have gone back to the beginning of this chapter and tackled those questions once again. Can you answer them now? When you have mastered those questions and answers you are ready to press onward.

FOR FURTHER STUDY

1. Study thoroughly the historical and religious background of the King James Version of 1611.

2. Prepare short biographies of the great men behind the English Bible (e.g., John Wycliffe and William Tyndale).

END NOTES

[1] Sakae Kubo and Walter Specht, *So Many Versions?* (Grand Rapids, MI: Zondervan Publishing House, 1975), pp.208-32.

[2] Gerald Hawthorne, "How to Choose a Bible." *Christianity Today*, Dec. 5, 1975, pp.7-10.

[3] *Ibid.,* p 8.

[4] Kubo and Specht, *So Many Versions?* p.199.

BIBLIOGRAPHY

Bruce, F.F. *The English Bible: A History of Translations from the Earliest English Versions to the New English Bible,* Revised Edition. Oxford University Press, 1970.

Douglas, J.D. (ed.). *The New International Dictionary of the Christian Church.* Grand Rapids, MI: Zondervan Publishing House, 1974.

Fuller, David Otis (ed.). *Which Bible?* Grand Rapids, MI: Grand Rapids International Publications, 1973.

Kubo, Sakae and Specht, Walter. *So Many Versions? Twentieth Century English Versions of the Bible.* Grand Rapids, MI: Zondervan Publishing House, 1983.

Lewis, Jack P. *The English Bible from KJV to NIV: A History and Evaluation.* Grand Rapids, MI: Baker Book House, 1982.

CHAPTER TEN

ঽ

ERRORS:
APPARENT OR REAL?

Preparing the Way

1. How can you ever reconcile Daniel 1:1, which asserts that Nebuchadnezzar attacked Jerusalem in the third year of the reign of Jehoiakim, with Jeremiah 25:1, which declares it took place in the fourth year?

2. How do you resolve the conflict between the very old age of man proposed by science and the very recent age of man presented in Scripture?

3. Matthew 1:8 speaks of Uzziah as the son of Joram. However the Old Testament (2 Kings 8:25; 11:2; 14:1,21) clearly teaches he was Joram's great-great-grandson. Is this not an error in the Bible? How do you explain it?

4. Moses is said to have written the book of Deuteronomy. Yet the final chapter contains the detailed account of his death and burial. How can this be? Is this not an anachronism?

5. Some biblical scholars have pin-pointed the date of the creation of the universe at 4004 B.C. The Bible is surely in error at this point, is it not?

6. How can you believe in inerrancy when 1 Kings 4:26 claims that Solomon had 40,000 stalls of horses, and 2 Chronicles 9:25 states he had only 4,000?

7. When the Bible speaks of the sun standing still, is it not using unscientific language that reflects the ignorance of the ancient Near East? How can you speak of inerrancy in the face of such an obvious scientific error?

8. Is there not a contradiction between the stance of the Old Testament on polygamy and the teaching of the New Testament on monogamy?

It is questions such as these that sow seeds of doubt in the minds of many sincere Christians. Do we have answers? Absolutely.

How well I remember the first time my faith was really threatened. It was in my senior year at a Canadian university. Although that won't surprise most of you, this may: the reliability of the Bible was questioned by a minister, a teacher of the Bible, a professor in the department of religion. That year I had chosen as an elective a course on the New Testament, not realizing I was stepping into Satan's stronghold. What a shock!

The first sign of a problem came when our scholarly professor eloquently held forth on Jesus' reaction in cursing the fig tree. He labelled it as our Lord's first great sin! In a fit of anger He cursed a tree for having no figs at a time of year before figs could be expected. That was only the beginning. Lecture after lecture was subtly seasoned with suggestions that were calculated to erode one's faith in the reliability of the Scriptures. He was a master at excavating "errors" in the Bible. Dozens of them were hurled at us. He seemed to delight in embarrassing the naive evangelical. The few of us in the class were made to look like simpletons.

Anachronisms and contradictions were surely there. But were they real errors or only apparent? For several months I pondered that question. It drove me to earnest prayer and careful study.

The problem is by no means recent. Nor is it limited to the experience of a few Christians. In 1800 the French Institute in Paris issued a list of eighty-two errors in the Bible, which they believed would lead to the death of Christianity. In his book, *The Bible: Its Origin and Nature,* Marcus Dods presents the six contradictions in the Gospels that led him to reject the doctrine of inerrancy.[1] The well-known archaeologist Sir Fredric Kenyon offers still another list of Bible contradictions.[2] Many readers will remember the disturbing effects of an article *Life* published some time ago entitled "5,000 Errors in the Bible."

We have already argued for the inerrancy of the original manuscripts. We have demonstrated the great reliability of our present English translations. How then, do we explain the contradictions and anachronisms in our Bible? Are the errors apparent or real? What are the evangelical's answers to the charge of errors and contradictions in our Bible?

A careful and unprejudiced examination of several of these "errors" will demonstrate not only that plausible and often conclusive explanations are available to us today, but that there are several basic propositions that summarize the orthodox answer to these difficulties.[3]

I. Incomplete Sources

PROPOSITION ONE: WE RECOGNIZE THAT EXTRA-BIBLICAL SOURCES ARE INCOMPLETE AND THEREFORE INCONCLUSIVE.

For a typical example of this proposition at work consider the apparent contradiction between Daniel 1:1 and Jeremiah 25:1.

> In the third year of the reign of Jehoiakim king of Judah, Nebuchadnezzar King of Babylon came to Jerusalem and besieged it. (Dan. 1:1)

> The word that came to Jeremiah concerning all the people of Judah, in the fourth year of Jehoiakim the son of Josiah, king of Judah (that was the first year of Nebuchadnezzar king of Babylon). (Jer. 25:1)

The problem is obvious. Daniel identifies the time of the invasion as the third year, while Jeremiah says it was the fourth year.

There is an explanation. Recent archaeological discoveries relevant to the time of Daniel have demonstrated that a Babylonian calendar existed alongside the Hebrew calendar. Between these two calendars there are major differences that bear upon our problem. The Hebrew calendar included the year of accession as the first year of the reign of a king. The Babylonian calendar did not consider the year of accession as the first year of his reign, but rather the first full year. Daniel, writing from Babylon, used the Babylonian calendar. Therefore he did not include the partial year of accession as the first year, and says the invasion occurred in the third year of Jehoiakim's reign. However, Jeremiah remained with the remnant in Jerusalem and therefore wrote using the Hebrew calendar. This made the year of accession the first year of the king's reign and places the invasion in the fourth year.[4]

Daniel	Jeremiah
Babylonian Calendar	Hebrew Calendar

```
        Daniel                    Jeremiah
   Babylonian Calendar        Hebrew Calendar

      Accession              ⌈ Accession
                           1 |
    ⌈ New Year               ⌊ New Year
  1 |
    ⌊ New Year             2 ⌈
  2 ⌈                        ⌊ New Year
    ⌊ New Year             3 ⌈
  3 ⌈                        ⌊ New Year
    ⌊ Invasion             3 ⌈
                             ⌊ Invasion
```

The principle here is obvious. For centuries it has been possible to set Daniel 1:1 against Jeremiah 25:1 and charge the Bible with an error. This charge rested upon the incomplete knowledge of the historians and critics. It stood until an archaeologist uncovered the fact of the two calendars and their differences. Now the "error" of Daniel 1:1 and Jeremiah 25:1 is eliminated. There is no problem whatsoever. It was only an apparent error.

Extra-biblical sources (history, archaeology, geology, anthropology, etc.) are incomplete. Although they have contributed a wealth of knowledge in a host of areas, yet these very areas are the subject of continual research. For this reason we must say these extra-biblical sources are not conclusive. It is estimated that a mere two percent of the potential archaeological work in the Bible lands has been done so far. Obviously the findings are incomplete and inconclusive. When someone charges the Bible with an error in the light of our present knowledge from history or archaeology, here is one possible line of defence. We confidently assert that it is only an apparent error. The validity of this principle has been demonstrated over and over again.

Few books have been so attacked as the prophecy of Daniel. Because "Belshazzar" was nowhere found in any extra-biblical material, for many years he was thought to be an unhistorical character. Here was one of the great "errors" in the Bible. But today his name is found on tablets that speak of him as "the son of the king." Now extra-biblical sources authenticate him as a historical person. A further problem existed in Daniel 5:1. Was Belshazzar, in fact, the last king of Babylon? Extra-biblical sources indicated it was Nabonidus. Again for many years this was labelled an error in the Scriptures. Today, however, the evidence is that Belshazzar reigned as second in command after his father, Nabonidus, went into semi-retirement in his Northern Arabian headquarters at Teman. This explains why Belshazzar offered Daniel the third place in the kingdom (Dan. 5:16) for interpreting the dream. He himself occupied the second place. Further light from extra-biblical sources have confirmed that he was, in fact, the last king of Babylon.[5] As the extra-biblical sources have become more complete, these alleged errors in the Book of Daniel have come to be recognized only as apparent errors. They appeared to be errors because our extra-biblical sources were incomplete.

These and hundreds more testify to the valid use of this proposition. Many of the problems that still remain can be labelled apparent errors and filed under this category. They appear to be errors because our information from extra-biblical sources is incomplete. If that information is incomplete, it is also inconclusive.

PROJECT NUMBER 1

1. Apply Proposition One to the following allegation. Because handwriting did not exist in the mid-second millennium B.C., Moses could not be the author of the first five books of our Bible.

2. What evidence is there from recent archaeological discoveries to support the Mosaic authorship of Genesis–Deuteronomy?[6]

II. Scientific Errors

PROPOSITION TWO: WE RECOGNIZE THAT EXTRA-BIBLICAL MATERIAL HAS BEEN WRONGLY INTERPRETED.

Many apparent conflicts between science and Scripture can be sorted into this compartment. One of the most frequently posed problems relates to the age of the human race. Science commonly traces the history of the human race back one hundred million years. The Bible seems to present him as a very recent creation. Doesn't the Bible contradict science here?

Orthodox Christianity realizes that people of great knowledge and skill have, nevertheless, made interpretations of natural and scientific phenomena and stated conclusions that have been proved to be incorrect in the light of later evidence or more thorough research.

The "Piltdown Man" was a hoax. The announcement of Charles Dawson and Arthur Smith Woodward, December 18, 1912, that human remains had been found in Piltdown was retracted on November 21, 1953, when it was announced to the world that it all was a hoax perpetrated by Dawson. The "Nebraska Man" turned out to be a pig. The "Neanderthal Man" is now acknowledged to have been as upright and intelligent as we are today. There is widespread debate among scientists as to whether the "Java Man" and "Peking Man" ought to be listed as ape or as man.[7]

A few years ago in its science section *Time* (May 17, 1971) reported that a leading anthropologist had found that the "Neanderthal Man" who has been used as an explicit evidence of Darwin's theory of evolution was not a sub-human being after all. Evidence now points to the effect that such "cave men" were not apish animals but actually a group of human beings who suffered severe vitamin deficiencies, thus causing the apish features. This definitely put a thorn in the theory of the evolutionist.

For two primary reasons one is quite justified in viewing the date of the human race as interpreted by science with some skepticism. First, the methods of dating are open to question. All methods are based on the presupposition of uniformitarianism, which considers that climatic conditions and rates of decomposition or deterioration have been uniform from the beginning. This presupposition ignores the biblical teaching of a universal flood, which obviously would destroy uniformitarianism. Also, these methods of dating fail to entertain the appearance of age that certainly was present in the creation of Genesis 1-2. That is, if creationism and the flood story are accepted, uniformitarianism is no longer a valid presupposition. Second, there is a great scarcity of fossil evidence for the age of the human race, a scarcity that is surprising in view of the massive abundance of fossils today. Someone has said, "Faith is the substance of fossils hoped for, and the evidence of links unseen."

The admission that extra-biblical sources have been wrongly interpreted recently came from a space expert with NASA. A friend of mine asked him if he thought the Bible agreed with science. He asked "Which Science? The Science of 1900 or 1920 or 1940 or 1960 or 1980?" He concluded by indicating that he would immediately begin to doubt the Bible if and when it ever totally agreed with science! Why? Because science is in a constant state of change.

The evidence on incorrect interpretations of natural and scientific dates in the past justifies the stand of orthodox Christianity. Even in the face of apparent errors and contradictions between science and the Bible, we stand fast upon the reliability of the Word of God. We remember that extra-biblical phenomena have been, and often still are wrongly interpreted. With this proposition the loyal defender of the faith may deflect many diabolical darts designed to destroy our faith and God's Word.

PROJECT NUMBER 2

How many other scientific interpretations of natural phenomena can you list that have recently proven to be incorrect?

III. An Incomplete Book

PROPOSITION THREE: WE RECOGNIZE THAT THE BIBLICAL RECORD IS INCOMPLETE AND ELLIPTICAL. THEREFORE, ON OCCASION IT GIVES THE APPEARANCE OF ERRORS AND OMISSIONS.

This explains the many problems similar to the one in Matthew 1:8: "And to Asa was born Jehoshaphat; and to Jehoshaphat, Joram; and to Joram, Uzziah."

This text seems to claim that Uzziah was the son of Joram. However the Old Testament clearly teaches he was the great-great-grandson (2 Kings 8:25; 11:2; 14:1,21). To some this presents a problem. The explanation is obvious. In the Old Testament, New Testament and secular literature of the ancient Near East, "the son of" simply means "a descendant of" and may omit several generations. Jehu, son of Nimshi, (2 Kings 9:20) was actually grandson (9:2). Christ was called "Son of David" (Matt. 9:27) although David lived more than one thousand years earlier. In John 8:39 the Jews said, "Abraham is our father," an elliptical statement bridging two thousand years. This same style is evident in the secular writings of the day too. King Tirhakah (680 B.C.) of Egypt honours "his father" Sesostris III (1800 B.C.) who lived twelve hundred years earlier.

What is the point here? We recognize the Scriptures are incomplete and elliptical. Occasionally this does give the appearance of error. Understanding this principle eliminates the apparent conflict between the 612 years from the Exodus to the dedication of Solomon's Temple, determined by adding up the lengths of reigns of the judges and the kings, and the 480 years of 1 Kings 6:1. These two numbers can be harmonized by realizing that the biblical record is often elliptical and that there was obviously more than one judge in existence at a time, located in different parts of the land.

Kitchen has demonstrated that a harmonization of the kings of Israel and Judah is impossible apart from recognizing there were co-regencies in those days. As in the case of the judges above, so in this case the biblical record leaves out the details of these synchronous reigns.[8] The biblical record is incomplete. All the details are not given.

The writers of Scripture were extremely selective in their choice of content. Under the guidance of the Holy Spirit, they included and excluded material in view of their specific purpose for writing. With this in mind, we will also be careful not to place too much value on arguments or lessons that are based on silence. This can be an extremely dangerous procedure, and has led to doctrinal perversions and practical excesses throughout the history of the church. Beware of arguments from silence. Beware of the elliptical nature of Scripture. By its very nature it sometimes gives the appearance of contradictions. Many apparent errors can be safely filed in this compartment. The incompleteness of the biblical record is the cause of the problem. If we had all the facts, the apparent error would be eliminated.

IV. Troublesome Illusions

PROPOSITION FOUR: WE RECOGNIZE THAT THE ORIGINAL TEXT HAS BEEN MODERNIZED FOR CLARIFICATION OR FOR THE SAKE OF COMPLETENESS, AND DOES GIVE THE ILLUSION OF AN ANACHRONISM.

What do we mean by an anachronism? It is simply an event placed out of its proper historic time. To say Lincoln flew to Gettysburg would be an anachronism. There were no planes in the nineteenth century. Modernization of the text of Scripture may, on occasion, give such illusions to us today.

Perhaps the most obvious illustration of this principle at work is in Deuteronomy 34, the account of the death and burial of Moses. How could this be written by Moses, the one who orthodox Christianity claims is the author of the book? Is this not an anachronism? Does this not require the rejection of the Mosaic authorship of Deuteronomy?

Certainly not. The most plausible explanation is that Joshua, the successor of Moses, collected the books Moses had written, and wrote an appropriate conclusion to them. Under the inspiration of the Holy Spirit, he wrote the obituary at the end of the writings of Moses. Joshua's completion of the writings of Moses in Deuteronomy does give the illusion of an anachronism.

This principle is seen elsewhere. In Genesis 11:31, Moses (writing in the fifteenth century B.C.) speaks of Ur of the Chaldees. However, this area in Mesopotamia was not so named Chaldea until the eleventh century. This does not mean that Genesis 11 was written after the eleventh century B.C. To say this would be to destroy the Mosaic authorship of Genesis. There is another explanation. After the fifteenth century B.C., a second city named Ur was built near Haran. Therefore it appears that at some later date "of Chaldees" was added in Genesis 11:31 to distinguish the Ur of Abraham's home from the new Ur north of Haran.

This same principle bears upon the name of the city built by the Israelites in bondage. If the exodus occurred around 1440 B.C., then the building of the city Ramses (Ex. 1:11) was shortly prior to this date. However, Ramses the Pharaoh, after whom the city was named, did not come to the throne until 1301 B.C. Does this mean the exodus occurred after 1301 B.C.? Not necessarily. There is another possibility. The text of Moses may well have been modernized by changing the name in Exodus 1:11 and recording the more modern name of the city.[9]

PROJECT NUMBER 3

1. Who may have modernized the text?

2. What is the difference between these "modernizations" and the intentional changes made by some scribes?

V. Interpretive Errors

PROPOSITION FIVE: WE FREELY ADMIT THAT THE BIBLICAL TEXT OFTEN HAS BEEN WRONGLY INTERPRETED.

It is commonly thought today that such was the case with James Ussher. He was the learned, seventeenth-century Anglican archbishop of Ireland who prepared a chronology of biblical events and reckoned that the creation of the universe occurred in 4004 B.C. Since the mid-nineteenth century this date has been rejected by scholars of science and Scripture. Students of the Bible have come to realize that the genealogies of Genesis 5 and 11, as well as those in 1 Chronicles, are not closed or tight genealogical records, but rather have some omissions. It is impossible to affirm the extent of the omissions or to fix absolute dates prior to Abraham.

In this case, as well as in many others, orthodox Christians admit that the Bible text has been and still may be wrongly interpreted. This accounts for many apparent contradictions between Scripture and history, geography or archaeology. The contradiction is due to an incorrect interpretation of the Bible.

PROJECT NUMBER 4

1. Discuss Israel's errors in interpreting the nature and mission of the Messiah (Luke 24:44,45), as well as the true nature of the Law (Matt. 5).

2. Discuss the erroneous interpretation of Job 9:6 by the Medieval Church.

Historically many apparent errors have simply been resolved with the admission that the error is ours in the interpretation of the Scriptures. May God ever give evangelical Christians the grace not only to refrain from dogmatic interpretations in matters of secondary importance, but also to admit their errors in interpretation when the facts demand it.

VI. Scribal Errors

PROPOSITION SIX: WE RECOGNIZE THAT ERRORS HAVE COME INTO THE TEXT THROUGH ITS TRANSMISSION.

Here is a typical example:

> And Solomon had 40,000 stalls of horses for his chariots, and 12,000 horsemen. (1 Kings 4:26)

> Now Solomon had 4,000 stalls for horses and chariots and 12,000 horsemen, and he stationed them in the chariot cities and with the king in Jerusalem. (2 Chron. 9:25)

One verse reads 40,000; another reads 4,000. This difficulty arose through the error of scribes in copying the text. The transmission of numerals was especially susceptible to error. In spite of the meticulous care of the scribes to preserve the text, errors did creep into the copies.

PROJECT NUMBER 5

1. Identify the textual problem between 1 Corinthians 10:8 and Numbers 25:9. What is the solution to this problem?

2. Identify the textual problem between 2 Samuel 8:4 and 1 Chronicles 18:4. Suggest a possible solution to the discrepancy.

Consider a slightly more complicated case. In Judges 18:30, some older manuscripts read "Moses." The Authorized Version follows the later manuscripts and reads "Manasseh." This may be the work of scribes who could not believe that a son of Moses would ever set up an idol as described in this verse. Probably they changed the name to Manasseh—simply the addition of one Hebrew letter.

Although many textual "errors" can be pointed out, it must always be remembered that providentially we have more manuscript evidence than any ancient literature to use in identifying and resolving such "errors." Also, the number of serious variants is so few they would fill only a page or two of our Bibles and none of these variants affect any doctrine of Scripture. Do not be influenced by those irrational critics who maliciously and unjustly scream that the Bible is full of errors.

VII. Optic Language

PROPOSITION SEVEN: WE RECOGNIZE THE USE OF PHENOMENAL LANGUAGE, WHICH GIVES THE APPEARANCE OF CONTRADICTIONS WITH SCIENCE.

Phenomenal language is the language of observation. It is optic language, stating the case as it appears to the eye.

Bernard Ramm explains:

> Its language about astronomy, botany, zoology and geology is
> restricted to the vocabulary of popular observation. What
> can be seen through a microscope or telescope is not com-
> mented on. Phenomenal language is true because all it claims
> is to be descriptive. One is not deceived when he sees the sun
> rise or the sun set. One is deceived only if he artlessly con-
> verts his observation into theories.[10]

Such language is frequently used in Scripture. Perhaps the best-known
illustration of this type of terminology is found in the record of the southern
campaign of Joshua's invasion of Canaan (Josh. 10). In response to Joshua's
prayer recorded in verse 13, we are told the "sun stood still." The daylight was
prolonged until the campaign was successfully completed. This statement has
been called the most striking incident of Scripture and science being at vari-
ance. Opponents of inerrancy ask, Does this verse not reflect the imperfect scientific knowledge of Joshua's day? They thought of their earth as the centre of
the universe and the sun rotating around the earth. Is this not an unscientific
statement and therefore an error?

Not necessarily so. C.F. Keil and F. Delitzsch explain the language here
when they write,

> Even the strictest and most literal interpretation of the words
> does not require us to assume, as the Fathers and earlier the-
> ologians did, that the sun itself was miraculously made to
> stand still, but simply supposes an *optical* stopping of the sun
> in its course—that is to say, a miraculous suspension of the
> revolution of the earth upon its axis, which would make it
> appear to the eye of the observer as if the sun itself were
> standing still.[11] (Emphasis added.)

That such language is quite legitimate is evident from the fact that every
almanac, newspaper and weather report still designates the time for the sunrise
and sunset!

Such optic language is common throughout Scripture. The atmospheric
heavens that surround the earth are described as a "firmament" in Genesis 1:6.
This noun comes from the Hebrew verb "to stretch" or "to spread out." Then
it came to mean "to beat, to hammer, to tread out." Hence the "firmament" is
the spreading out of the air around the earth as an atmosphere. This is optic
language.

PROJECT NUMBER 6
Study the following verses to discover their use of phenomenal language. How
is the atmosphere described in each verse?

Psalm 104:2   Isaiah 40:22   Job 37:18

VIII. Progressive Revelation

PROPOSITION EIGHT: WE RECOGNIZE THE FACT OF PROGRESSIVE REVE-
LATION, WHICH GIVES THE APPEARANCE OF CONTRADICTION BETWEEN
THE OLD AND NEW TESTAMENTS, OR EVEN BETWEEN EARLIER AND
LATER WRITERS.

In the Old Testament era polygamy was widely practised. It was never condemned openly by God. He seemed to tolerate it at least. In the New
Testament era monogamy is taught more clearly. Often Bible teachers are
asked, Is this not a contradiction between the Old and New Testament?

Although polygamy was not explicitly condemned in the Old Testament,
neither was it directly approved by God. Some suggest that Israel in the Old
Testament era was in ethical and theological infancy, and did not come to
maturity until the New Testament times. Support for this may be found in the
transition from law in the Old Testament to grace in the New Testament—a
transition that is appropriate for people moving from immaturity to maturity.
In the period of their infancy, God tolerated certain things that He did not
tolerate in their maturity. In growing from infancy to maturity there was a
raising of ethical standards and an advance in theological knowledge. Whether
or not this explanation is acceptable or correct, the fact remains that there was
a progression in God's revelation throughout the history covered by the Bible.

Such progress in revelation is more apparent perhaps in regard to the doctrine
of the Trinity. Throughout the Old Testament there are merely intimations of a tri-
une Godhead. In the New Testament it is explicit. There is no contradiction.

PROJECT NUMBER 7

How is the principle of progressive revelation demonstrated in the following
verses?

    Ephesians 3:1-12   1 Timothy 3:8 ff.   1 Thessalonians 4:16-18

There is progress in the revelation given by God. Many "errors" dissolve
merely into apparent errors under the scrutiny of this important proposition.

IX. Unresolved Difficulties

These principles will be useful to resolve most of the apparent contradictions
and anachronisms. Learn them well. When a problem is raised, ask yourself
under which category it fits. Most will be easily fitted. However, these do not
remove all the difficulties. In facing the unresolved difficulties, we ought to
keep in mind three very important points.

First, the burden of proof is upon the critic to prove that the difficulty is
indeed an error. The Bible claims to be the inerrant Word of God. It has been
universally accepted as such for centuries. That claim stands until it is proven
otherwise. The burden of proof is on the critic. We simply say, "Prove it."

Second, a difficulty remains only a difficulty and does not move into the category of an error until it is proven unequivocally to be an error. This "proof" cannot merely be alleged on ambiguous grounds. B.B. Warfield writes:

> Every unharmonized passage remains a case of difficult harmony and does not pass into the category of objections to plenary inspiration. It can pass into the category of objections only if we are prepared to affirm that we clearly see that it is, on any conceivable hypothesis of its meaning, clearly inconsistent with the biblical doctrine of inspiration.[12]

To say the Bible contradicts science is to say that we know all about geology and anthropology, that all the archaeological evidence is in and that we accurately and completely understand the Bible. This is a very precarious, if not impossible stance to assume. Who would dare to make such a claim?

To say one verse contradicts another is to presuppose that we have all the facts on the two verses. As you can see, therefore, the person who claims the Bible is in error is making an arrogant claim of virtual omniscience. A critic is compelled to substantiate any such criticism with complete and conclusive evidence.

Dr. Robert Dick Wilson, a Hebrew professor at Princeton Seminary, was a world-renowned scholar. He knew and spoke more than forty-five languages and dialects. Yet he once said, "No man knows enough to disprove the inspiration, accuracy and authority of the Bible." Hear him again, "Gentlemen, those things which I do not understand in the Bible, I put down to my own ignorance." What a remarkably humble posture.

> Every word of God is tested: He is a shield to those who take refuge in Him. Do not add to His words, lest He reprove you, and you be proved a liar. (Prov. 30:5,6)

The third important point to be remembered is that the history of alleged errors is on the side of orthodox evangelical Christianity. In 1800 the French Institute listed its eighty-two errors that were to destroy the Bible. Today every one of them has been satisfactorily answered. The great liberal critic Wellhausen knew of no domesticated camels at the time of Abraham, Isaac and Jacob. Therefore, he concluded, Genesis could not have been written by Moses as the Bible claims. He denied the unity of the Pentateuch and disputed its Mosaic authorship. Today archaeology has provided us with coins showing domesticated camels even before the biblical dating of the patriarchs! He spoke on the basis of incomplete and inconclusive extra-biblical sources. Plausible explanations have been offered for most of Marcus Dods' and Sir Frederic Kenyon's troublesome contradictions.

Though Clark Pinnock has become more liberal in his view of inerrancy, he correctly points out that the Bible has often been unjustly attacked. A century ago the book of Genesis was considered a hopeless collection of unsubstantiated myths. Moses, it was thought, would have been unable to write.

The Hittites had never existed. The literature was put together with scissors and paste at the hands of fairly unintelligent ancient bookmakers. Then the avalanche of discovery in the Near East came to bury these preposterous theories. Egyptian and Hittite parallels turned up in abundance. Personal names and customs were found echoed in the Amarna letters, the Nuzi tablets and the Ugaritic texts. The fanciful criteria for discerning literary strands in the documents of the Pentateuch have been subjected to severe criticism and abandoned by many. Writing in the Near East was already a well-established art in the second millennium B.C. If critics continue to point to Genesis with allegations of "error," they will do so despite the evidence, not because of it.[13]

I once heard of a history class that was studying the French Revolution. For a particular assignment they were asked to report on the vote that condemned Louis XVI to death. One half of the class reported that the vote was unanimous. Some of the students reported it was a majority of one. A few declared it was a majority of one hundred forty-five in the total vote of seven hundred and twenty-one.

At first sight this looks like a hopeless contradiction. As a matter of fact, all three reports were accurate. You see, actually three votes were taken. On the issue of his guilt, the vote was unanimous. On the issue of his sentence, he was condemned to die by a majority of one hundred forty-five. On the issue of his immediate execution, the decision was passed by a majority of one.

When all the facts are in there is no contradiction! So also with the Word of God. The more the facts become available, the fewer the unresolved difficulties and the stronger the inerrancy of Scripture. It becomes obvious to us then, that if all the facts were in, the supposed contradictions in the synoptic Gospels would quickly disappear, and with them all the others as well.

In the meantime, difficulties do still remain! We cannot resolve all the difficulties. We cannot hope to ever do this as long as our extra-biblical sources are incomplete or subject to wrong interpretations, and as long as we bear the limitations of finite minds. How shall we respond in the face of the questions we can't answer, the difficulties we can't resolve?

> Difficulties in Scripture do not deny inspiration nor destroy inerrancy. They are but mountains yet to be scaled and lands yet to be conquered.[14]

Review

1. List from memory the eight propositions of this chapter.

2. Turn back to the questions at the beginning of this chapter. Each problem is solved by the application of one of these propositions. Can you match the appropriate proposition to each problem?

END NOTES

1 Marcus Dods, *The Bible: Its Origin and Nature* (New York, NY: C. Scribner's Sons, 1905), pp.136,137.

2 Sir Fredric Kenyon, *The Bible and Archaeology* (New York, NY: Harper and Row, 1940), p.27.

3 I am greatly indebted to Dr. Bruce Waltke who, while teaching at Dallas Theological Seminary, not only exposed me to many of these principles, but also strengthened my faith in the Scriptures by his scholarly application of them to the Old Testament.

4 Gleason L. Archer Jr., *A Survey of Old Testament Introduction* (Chicago, IL: Moody Press, 1964), p.369.

5 John F. Walvoord, *Daniel* (Chicago, IL: Moody Press, 1971), pp.113-15.

6 K.A. Kitchen, *Ancient Orient and Old Testament* (Chicago, IL: InterVarsity Press, 1966), p.20, pp.92-102.

7 Bolton Davidheisser, *Evolution and Christian Faith* (Philadelphia, PA: The Presbyterian and Reformed Publishing Company, 1969), pp.330-349.

8 K.A. Kitchen, *Ancient Orient and Old Testament,* p.63.

9 For another explanation of the name of this city, see Gleason Archer, *A Survey of Old Testament Introduction,* p.207.

10 Bernard Ramm, *Protestant Biblical Interpretation* (Boston, MA: W.A. Wilde Company, 1956), p.191.

11 C.F. Keil and F. Delitzsch, *Biblical Commentary on the Old Testament— Joshua, Judges, Ruth* (Grand Rapids, MI: Wm. B. Eerdmans Publishing Company, 1963), p.112.

12 B.B. Warfield, *The Inspiration and Authority of the Bible* (Philadelphia, PA: The Presbyterian and Reformed Publishing Company, 1970), p.220.

13 Clark Pinnock, *Set Forth Your Case* (Nutley, NJ: The Craig Press, 1968), p.71.

14 *Ibid.,* p.73.

BIBLIOGRAPHY

Archer, Gleason L. *A Survey of Old Testament Introduction.* Chicago, IL: Moody Press, 1964.

Bruce, F.F. *Are the New Testament Documents Reliable?* London: The InterVarsity Fellowship, 1950.

Davidheisser, Bolton. *Evolution and Christian Faith.* Philadelphia, PA: The Presbyterian and Reformed Publishing Company, 1969.

Dods, Marcus. *The Bible: Its Origin and Nature.* New York, NY: C. Scribner's Sons, 1905.

Keil, C.F. and Delitzsch, F. *Biblical Commentary on the Old Testament—Joshua, Judges, Ruth.* Grand Rapids, MI: Wm. B. Eerdmans Publishing Company, 1963.

Kenyon, Sir Fredric. *The Bible and Archaeology.* New York, NY: Harper and Row, 1940.

Kitchen, K.A. *Ancient Orient and Old Testament.* Chicago, IL: InterVarsity Press, 1966.

Lindsell, Harold. *The Battle for the Bible.* Grand Rapids, MI: Zondervan Publishing House, 1976.

Pinnock, Clark. *A Defense of Biblical Infallibility.* Philadelphia, PA: Presbyterian and Reformed Publishing Company, 1967.

— *Set Forth Your Case.* Nutley, NJ: The Craig Press, 1968.

Ramm, Bernard. *Protestant Biblical Interpretation.* Boston, MA: W.A. Wilde Company, 1956.

Walvoord, John F. *Daniel.* Chicago, IL: Moody Press, 1971.

Warfield, B.B. *The Inspiration and Authority of the Bible.* Philadelphia, PA: The Presbyterian and Reformed Publishing Company, 1970.

Young, Edward J. *Thy Word Is Truth.* Grand Rapids, MI: Wm. B. Eerdmans Publishing Company, 1967.

CHAPTER ELEVEN

৯

A BOOK TO LIVE BY

The law of the Lord is perfect,
restoring the soul;

The testimony of the Lord is sure
making wise the simple.

The precepts of the Lord are right,
rejoicing the heart;

The commandment of the Lord is pure,
enlightening the eyes.

The fear of the Lord is clean,
enduring forever;

The judgments of the Lord are true;
they are righteous altogether.

They are more desirable than gold,
yes, than much fine gold;

Sweeter also than honey and the
drippings of the honeycomb. (Ps. 19:7-10)

Robert G. Lee, well-known author and Bible conference speaker, president of the Southern Baptist Convention for three consecutive years, tells the remarkable story of an exceedingly costly jewel that for many years was considered of no more value than a mere pebble:

> Gustaf Gillman, a Chicago lapidary was at work in his shop, according to the narrative, when John Mihok of Omaha entered. Mihok, who was a laborer, drew out of his pocket a rough red stone and handed it to Gillman and said, "I want you to cut and polish this."
>
> "Where did you get it?" gasped Gillman, as his eyes almost popped out of his head.
>
> "My father picked it up in Hungary fifty years ago," was the reply of Mihok. "He thought it was a pretty pebble. When I landed in this country, I found it in my valise. It has been lying around the house ever since. The children played with it. My last baby cut his teeth on it. One night, I dreamed it was a diamond and worth a lot of money, but it's not a diamond. It's red."
>
> "No, it's a pigeon's blood ruby," said Gillman.
>
> "What might it be worth?" was the question of Mihok.
>
> "I'd say anywhere from $100,000 to $250,000," answered Gillman; Mihok leaned against the door.
>
> The big, rough stone, we are told, cut to a flawless ruby of 23 9/10ths carats. It is believed to be the largest ruby in this country and possibly the largest in the world.[1]

How tragic that the Book that is infinitely more valuable than a thousand jewels is considered of so little value by so many today! Hopefully, the study of the making of the Bible has enhanced the value of the Book to you, and increased your appreciation of its infinite worth.

The ultimate test of its value is in its practical impact on your personal life. To conclude our study, let us consider several of the prominent purposes of the Scriptures.

I. It Leads Men and Women to Christ

First, and foremost, this is the Book that leads men and women to God. The great English translator, William Tyndale, boldly declared:

> The Scripture is that wherewith God draweth us unto Him, and not wherewith we should be led from Him. The

Scriptures spring out of God, and flow unto Christ, and were given to lead us to Christ. Thou must therefore go along by the Scripture as by a line, until thou come to Christ, which is the way's end and resting place.

This statement stands the test of Scripture itself (Luke 24:27; John 5:39). Is it not through this that you have come to know, trust and love your Saviour? The fulfilling of this purpose alone renders the Bible a priceless Book.

PROJECT NUMBER 1

1. Who is the central subject of all the Scripture? (John 5:39; Luke 24:27).

2. What are the Scriptures able to do? (2 Tim. 3:15; John 3:16).

3. Of what may one be absolutely assured through the Scriptures? (John 6:37, 10:28-30; 1 John 5:11-13).

II. It Equips the Christian Worker

All Scripture is inspired by God and profitable for teaching, for reproof; for correction, for training in righteousness; that the man of God may be adequate, equipped for every good work. (2 Tim. 3:16,17)

PROJECT NUMBER 2

The profit of the Scriptures extends into four areas. Consider each of these carefully. What is the specific use of Scripture in each of these four areas?

Teaching –

Reproof –

Correction –

Training in righteousness –

The orderly sequence of this verse may be viewed from still another perspective. The "teaching" acquaints us with the truth. The "conviction" or "reproof" makes us aware of our failure to live up to the truth. In its "improvement" or "correction" it shows us how to eliminate the failures thus exposed. Its "training" is the total education in holiness, which is the result of the first three levels.

Not only is it profitable, however, it is also sufficient. If our text is to be taken seriously, the Scriptures are sufficient to equip us fully for any service for our Master. If you know the Bible as you ought to know it and as God intends you to know it, you are equipped to do anything God wants you to do. The person who knows the Word is adequate. He is equipped for every good work.

III. It Arms the Christian Warrior

> And take the helmet of salvation, and the sword of the Spirit,
> which is the word of God. (Eph. 6:17)

The sword of the Spirit is the Word of God. It will be extremely helpful to make a fine distinction here between two Greek words. Both are translated "word" in our English Bible, but they must not be confused. In Hebrews 4:12 the Bible is designated as the *logos* of God while in our text, Ephesians 6:17, it is called the *rhema* of God. *Logos* refers to the Bible as a whole, to the written word of God. *Rhema* is a much more technical, restrictive term. In Luke 3:2 it is used in a solemn sense of a particular word of the Lord that came to the heart of John the Baptist. It is used of a Christian confession or a preached word in Romans 10:8,9 and Ephesians 5:20. A definite, specific, preached utterance is classified as a *rhema* in John 6:63.

In Ephesians 6:17, the *rhema* of God bears three distinctives.

A. A Spoken Word Appropriate to the Situation

When an overwrought parent says to her two scrapping children, "Blessed are the peacemakers," she is using the Scriptures as the *rhema* of God. When a frustrated embittered Christian reminds himself, "Be ye kind one to another…," he is using the Bible as the *rhema* of God. When a teenager faced with a temptation to disobey her parents is confronted by, "Children obey your parents in the Lord," she is feeling the thrust of the *rhema* of God. How important it is to know the Word of God. Cultivate a working knowledge of this Book. Memorize it. It is the *rhema* of God, the spoken word, which is peculiarly appropriate to the situation. It is the sword of the Spirit in your spiritual warfare.

B. An Authoritative Word

It is a spoken appropriate word that carries with it all the authority of God. It is the *rhema* of God. Never forget that Satan and his demonic forces remain subject to that authority even today. In the midst of a spiritual conflict, you have at your disposal an arsenal of appropriate words that, if but spoken to the enemy, will subdue him. He is subject to the authority behind that word. It was the realization of this great truth that prompted Luther to write:

> And let the prince of ill
> Look grim as ever he will
> He harms us not a whit
> A *Word* shall quickly slay him. (Emphasis added.)

It is pure folly to leave the security and safety of the authoritative Word of God to engage the archenemy of your soul in open combat. Defeat is certain. Learn the Word. Study it. Memorize it. Use it. Then trust in it! If you aspire to victory, confide in the authority of the Word of God. It alone is adequate for the foe we face.

C. An Acquired Word

We receive it from the Holy Spirit. It is the "sword of the Spirit." Students of the language will call this a genitive of source. It proceeds from the Holy Spirit. He puts the sword into the hands of the believer. He provides the appropriate text. He does this in our witnessing, in our prayer life, and also in our spiritual warfare. It is acquired from the Holy Spirit at the time of combat. The Holy Spirit brings to the mind of the Christian in the midst of the crisis the very text that is appropriate for the situation.

But can He do this, or will He do this apart from our having learned the text in advance? Hardly. As we read, study and memorize Scripture, we store in the files of our minds the great texts that will be appropriate for any situation and serve in our spiritual warfare. As we are walking in fellowship with the Lord, His Holy Spirit supplies us with the needed weapons from the arsenal stored in our minds.

Computers today can record the entire Bible in one-sixth of a second. On command they can reproduce any verse in two-billionths of a second. This gives us some idea of the capability of the human brain under the impulse of the Spirit of God. From what has been stored there by study and meditation, He can recall and place in our hands for our spiritual defence.

How important it is then, to protect our communion with the Holy Spirit. A healthy relationship with the Spirit of God through confession and submission is an imperative for all who yearn for victory. He is the One who puts the sword in our hands!

If I see the verse correctly then, the successful offence of the Christian is by means of acquiring through the Holy Spirit an authoritative word that is appropriate to the particular temptation of Satan.

F.F. Bruce helpfully states, "the *rhema* is that utterance of God appropriate to the occasion which the Spirit, so to speak, puts into the hand of the believer to be wielded as a sword which will put his spiritual assailants to flight."[2]

This is the biblical means of resisting the devil.

Weapon
An Appropriate Word
An Authoritative Word
An Acquired Word

Means
Cultivate your knowledge of the Bible.
Confide in the authority of the Bible.
Commune with the Supplier of the Bible.

PROJECT NUMBER 3

1. Our Lord is the perfect example for every believer in every area of life. Read Matthew 4:1-11.
   a) How do you account for our Lord's victory over Satan?
   b) How is each of the three answers of our Lord introduced? Which aspect of the *rhema* is emphasized by this phrase?
   c) Demonstrate the appropriateness of each of the three "words" answered by our Lord.
   d) How do you suppose He acquired these three obscure verses hidden in Deuteronomy?

2. Eve is a shameful example of failure and defeat. In view of what you have learned of the *rhema* of God in Ephesians 6:17, how do you account for her fall before Satan?

IV. It Guides the Christian Pilgrim

No single category of questions plagues the minds of believers more, and is posed to pastors more often, than questions related to God's guidance. This is a constant concern for every conscientious Christian. And rightly so. Yet there is hope and help for such Christians in the Word of God.

To each of us is given the sure promise of divine guidance.

> Trust in the Lord with all your heart, And do not lean on your own understanding, In all your ways acknowledge Him, And He will make your paths straight. (Prov. 3:5,6)

Again to each of us has been given a gracious and adequate provision for our guidance.

> Thy Word is a lamp to my feet, And a light to my path. (Ps. 119:105)

What a glorious provision! He has given us the Book to guide us through life. The acid test to apply to any prospective course of action is this: Is it in obedience to the Word of God?

But how shall we use the Bible to obtain guidance? This is a question I am frequently asked. No doubt you have wondered about this very point. How is it to be used? Perhaps a few brief principles will be of some practical help.[3]

First, do not conduct a random search through the Bible for some proof text to give you direction.

Have you read of the man who was seeking guidance by closing his eyes, opening the Bible at random, putting his finger on the page, and then opening his eyes to read the text? The first text he chose told him Judas went out and hanged himself. Unhappy with the result he tried again. This time he fingered the verse which said, "Go, thou, and do likewise." More discontented than before, he tried a third time. He was shocked to read, "What thou doest, do quickly." This would surely be enough to cause anyone to abandon such a reckless and irresponsible procedure. The Bible was never intended to be used this way.

Second, do not resort to Scripture for guidance only at the time of the dilemma.

Actually the dilemma will test the depth of your regular systematic study of the Bible. The biblical message needs to be planted into the very depths of our thinking and attitudes so that it can percolate there and become a part of us, so that our real selves will be formed by it.

Third, we are to act on the biblical principles that govern life's large blocks. Here it is again. "Principlize." This will assist in moving from Paul's life to yours, from the interpretation to the application.

Fourth, be true always to the context. Never be guided by a text or a principle that is not true to its context.

Fifth, always remember that the Bible as a source of guidance does not eliminate the element of struggle. Apart from the struggles of discerning His mind, there would be little prayer, less growth and no sifting of priorities and values. It is for the cultivation of these rare and precious virtues that God schedules for His children those days and weeks of oppressive and agonizing struggle.

PROJECT NUMBER 4

Study the following texts. What is the particular contribution of each one to the subject of guidance and discerning the will of God?

1. Psalm 37:4,5

2. Colossians 3:15

3. Romans 12:1,2

4. James 1:5

5. Proverbs 3:5,6

V. It Accomplishes in the Believer Sanctification

"Sanctify them in the truth; Thy word is truth." (John 17:17)

The progressive sanctification of the Christian is his progressive growth into the likeness of Christ. It is his progressively being set apart for His use as His possession. It is the work God is doing in us today. And what is the means? The Word of God!

There is no verse in all Scripture that indicates the great importance of the Word of God to our spiritual life better than this text. But how does it accomplish this result? How do the Scriptures sanctify?

As a believer is exposed to truths of Scripture, as a person assimilates them, personally studies and develops proficiency in using the Scriptures, the Holy Spirit will be progressively moulding the person and setting the person apart as God's possession for God's use.

A child of God in the world is like a diver in the depths of the sea. One is pressed in on every side by evil—almost overwhelmed by it. The existence of the diver depends upon the diving suit. And what that suit is to the diver, the Word of God is to us. It keeps us from the evil. It separates us unto God. How utterly indispensable it is to our daily existence and growth.

In his *Lectures to My Students*, C.H. Spurgeon shows how anecdotes and illustrations may be used to explain a great story:

> A woman is called upon by her minister on Monday, and he finds her washing wool in a sieve, holding it under the pump. He asks her, "How did you enjoy last Sabbath's discourses?" She does not recollect, "What was the subject?" "Ah! sir, it was quite gone from me," says the poor woman. Does she remember any of the remarks that were made? No, they are all gone. "Well then, Mary," says the minister, "it could not have done you much good." Oh, but it had done her a great deal of good; and she explained it to him by saying, "I will tell you, sir, how it is; I put this wool in the sieve under the pump, I pump on it and all the water runs through the sieve, but then it washes the wool. So it is with your sermon; it comes into my heart, and then it runs right through my poor memory, which is like a sieve, but it washes me clean, sir."
>
> You might talk for a long while about the cleansing and sanctifying power of the Word, and it would not make such an impression upon your hearers as that simple story would.[4]

This Bible is the most precious piece of property possessed by any believer today. Treasure it above all else. Read it. Study it. Memorize it. Share it. But most of all, live it.

PROJECT NUMBER 5

Set for yourself several goals for your personal devotional reading of the Scripture. They should be specific and direct. Make them realistic enough that they can be attained, yet difficult enough that they will stretch you. We should have both short-range and long-range goals.

1.

2.

3.

4.

5.

END NOTES

[1] Robert G. Lee, *By Christ Compelled* (Grand Rapids, MI: Zondervan Publishing House, 1969). p.49.

[2] F.F. Bruce, *The Epistle to the Ephesians* (Westwood, NJ: Fleming H. Revell Company, 1961), p.131.

[3] For further study consider carefully the article by Montagu Barker entitled "How the Bible Helps You Make Decisions," *How to Study the Bible,* ed. John B. Job (InterVarsity Press), pp. 90-98.

[4] C.H. Spurgeon, *Lectures to My Students* (Grand Rapids, MI: Zondervan Publishing House, 1954), pp.385,386.

BIBLIOGRAPHY

Bruce, F.F. *The Books and the Parchments: Some Chapters on the Transmission of the Bible,* third ed. Westwood, NJ: Fleming H. Revell Company, 1963.

Greenslade, S.L. (ed. et al). *Cambridge History of the Bible.* Cambridge: The University Press, 1963-1970.

Herklots, H.G.G. *How Our Bible Came to Us.* Oxford University Press, 1954.

Metzger, Bruce and Coogan, Michael D. *The Oxford Companion to the Bible.* Oxford University Press, 1993.